MW01701110

Resisting Retirement

5 Reasons You're Ready and You Just Didn't Know It!

Jaclyn Scott

Table of Contents

Introduction

Do you remember the tingle of excitement during the last days of school—the way the air pulsed with the promise of freedom and endless summer days? Those long hours of leisure seemed to stretch out before you like an open road destined for adventure. Now imagine capturing that very same feeling as an adult—except this time, it isn't a break that lasts for a season; it's the beginning of an entirely new stage of life called retirement, the grand summer of your life's calendar.

Let's talk about Suzie. At 65, the countdown to her retirement felt like someone had lit a slow-burning fuse to a fireworks display. Every passing day was a step closer to what felt like an exciting yet somewhat daunting explosion of free time. Suzie's work life was her identity for more than four decades—she was the first to arrive, the last to leave, and always sandwiched a mere 30-minute lunch break between relentless waves of emails and calls.

Suzie was meticulous; her retirement fund resembled a carefully cultivated garden, each dollar planted with the hope it would bloom at retirement. But when "later" became "now," she faced a kaleidoscope of emotions. When she signed her retirement papers, Suzie worried that the freedom awaiting her might just be a rosy mirage. Perhaps it whispered something she feared to acknowledge—was retiring an admission that she was growing old?

Those initial weeks post-retirement were a strange cocktail of emotions for Suzie. Mornings, once defined by buzzing alarm clocks, were now ushered in by the gentle sunlight caressing her face. Her cherished second cup of coffee no longer sat trapped within the sterile confines of a desk corner; it was now savored on her front porch with the melodious chirping of birds and whispers of the neighborhood as her new playlist.

Suzie took walks—long, aimless walks—the kind where your feet take the lead, and your mind clears with every step. Days melted into each other without the urgency of schedules. The first sprouts of understanding began to emerge. Retirement was not about wilting away; it was about the blossoming of a new phase, rich and ripe with the freedom to slow dance with life's subtler rhythms. It didn't imply 'old'; instead, it beckoned 'bold' new experiences. She was an explorer, charting the unmapped territory of her newfound liberty.

Now, let's talk about retirement in simple terms. It's not every day that life hands you a blank slate and says, "Here you go; do whatever you want with your time." Well, that's what retirement is all about. It's the reward you get after years of juggling work, family, and all the little things in between. When you retire, every day is yours to shape. You wake up without the alarm. You sit at the breakfast table and actually hear the birds chirping outside because you're not in a rush. You're in control now, and that feels nice.

Think about all those things you've put on a shelf because of work. Maybe it's diving into books that have been collecting dust on your bookshelf, or it's tinkering with that old car in the garage that you promised yourself you'd fix up someday. Retirement is your chance to take those off the shelf and dive in.

Travel is another thing people look forward to in retirement. It doesn't have to be extravagant trips around the world—unless that's your thing. It could be as simple as road trips to places you've never been in your own country. The point is that you get to explore on your own terms without worrying about getting back to work.

Now, money. It's an important part of the equation, but it doesn't have to rule your life. You've likely been planning for this, and it's time to see your savings and pensions work for you. You don't need to be rich to enjoy retirement. It's all about living within your means and making smart choices so you can do the things that make you happy.

Speaking of happiness, retirement is a great time to give back. Whether it's volunteering at a local charity or helping out with the grandkids, it's about making a difference in the lives of others, and that can be very fulfilling.

Health is another priority for retirees. Without the daily grind, you can focus more on taking care of yourself. Maybe join a walking group, hit the local pool, or just set a routine for regular exercise—it will improve your quality of life. And for those days when you just want to relax, that's okay too. It's your time now. If you want to spend a day watching your favorite shows or puttering in the garden, that's your call. Retirement is about having the freedom to do as much or as little as you want.

Lastly, let's talk about community because it's more important than ever in retirement. It's wonderful to have friends and family with whom to share your time, whether it's regular catch-ups or the occasional get-together.

Retirement is a big change, but it's also a new chapter with the potential to be as fulfilling and exciting as the rest of your life has been. It's a time to enjoy the fruits of years of hard work without the pressure of a 9 to 5. So think about what you want from it and go for it. It's your time to shine in whatever way you choose.

I'm writing this book for all of you out there who, like my parents, are standing on the edge of retirement, feeling hesitant. My folks are in their golden years, and let me tell you, no one has worked harder. Despite this, they're not quite sure about taking the plunge. They worry they're not financially set, and they dread the thought of cutting back on the life they love. They deserve so much more than worry in the next act of their lives, don't you think?

It's not easy to step away from the rhythm of a working life that's played like a persistent drumbeat for decades. It's even harder when you're not sure if the music will keep playing. But here's the truth I've seen: retirement can be an incredible time of renewal and joy, and I've written this book to prove it.

I understand the fear. I see the uncertainty. That's why I've put my heart and soul into this book. I want to show my folks—and anyone who might feel the same—that there's a world of possibilities after retirement, one that doesn't require a mountain of gold to enjoy. Retirement can and should be a time of celebration, a period when you can finally take off your watch and live by what feels right.

In this book, I aim to guide you through the maze of retirement decisions. From managing your finances without losing sleep to finding new hobbies that spark joy rather than drain your wallet, I'll be with you every step of the way.

Let's talk financial readiness—it's always the elephant in the room. I'm going to show you how to look at what you have and make the most of it so you don't feel like you're stepping off a ledge. I've gathered practical advice and straightforward strategies to help protect what you've earned and maximize your pension, social security, and savings. You've built a life's work; now, let's make sure it supports you.

Of course, money isn't everything. Retirement is also about time—the one commodity you've never seemed to have enough of. Now's the chance to write a personal wish list that's all about time spent, not money. We'll explore new activities that cost little but enrich a lot. Imagine the joy of learning something new just because you can. That's the kind of spirit I want to capture.

Health is another focus. I'll share insights and tips on how you can invest in your well-being for a vibrant and energetic retirement. And then there's the social side of life—staying connected, making new friends, and maintaining a support network. Isolation is a common fear among retirees, but it doesn't have to be your reality. There are communities and social scenes emerging just for retirees, ripe and ready for you to join.

One of the most beautiful aspects of retiring is the chance to give back—to family, friends, or community causes that have always tugged at your heartstrings. I'll show you how helping others can be a huge part of your new routine without taking over your hard-earned freedom.

Retirement is also about knowing you don't have to jam-pack every day with activities. It's about the peace that comes with simply being without feeling idle or unproductive. I'll help you learn how to embrace this slower pace and find contentment every day.

Back to my parents—they are just like you—good, hard-working people who've earned every second of the reprieve that retirement affords. They've spent years caring for others; now it's time to care for themselves. Through this book, I'm aiming to not only offer guidance but also a hefty dose of encouragement. I want to show them and you the myriad of ways life can bloom after the full-time job ends.

While writing these pages, I've been thinking about those who've gone before, those brave souls.

Whether you're five years away from retirement or standing right on the diving board ready to jump, this book is a helping hand, a source of comfort, and a tool for planning. I'm here to tell you from the heart that retirement isn't the end—it's just a beautiful beginning, and you're more than ready to embrace it. Who's retired and navigated the changes with grace and verve? Their stories are here, full of honest advice and heartfelt reflections.

My ultimate goal is to give you a candid look at retirement that balances reality with optimism. You've spent a lifetime learning the ropes of your career; now it's time to enjoy the fruits of your labor, find new pursuits to cherish, and find ways to stay engaged and connected without breaking the bank.

Chapter 1:

You've Dreamed of a Life of Leisure—Isn't it Time to See the World?

The golden years of retirement unfold a new chapter in life where the days of the clock-in and clock-out routine dissolve into the freedom of endless possibility. It's a time when the daily hustle of a nine-to-five life fades into the background, leaving a clear horizon ahead. With this newfound freedom, retirement can be transformed into an exciting phase that's not just about unwinding but also about seizing the chance for delightful discoveries and experiences that have been shelved during the bustle of working years.

This period in life offers a unique opportunity to finally tackle that bucket list that has been gathering dust. Now, there's ample time to research those dream destinations, learn a few phrases in a new language, and dive into cultural immersions that were once confined to quick weekend getaways or travel brochures. These cultural immersions can broaden your horizons, deepen your understanding of the world, and improve mental agility. Unlike vacation time during our working lives, retirement allows for spontaneous decisions—deciding on a whim to see the vivid tulip fields of the Netherlands in full bloom or the northern lights in Iceland without the need to pencil in dates months in advance or to synchronize with a work calendar.

However, this freedom also requires a mental shift. Without the structure of a daily job, retirees must learn to navigate the expanse of free time that opens before them. It's not uncommon to feel unmoored initially as the previous routine falls away, leaving days wide open for personal pursuits. The key is to transition gracefully into this new pace of life, harnessing the unbounded time to fulfill long-held aspirations.

One might wonder, though, how to begin organizing such aspirations. Setting travel goals is a good start. These could range from visiting grandchildren across the country to exploring the ancient ruins of Machu Picchu. What's important is identifying places and experiences that resonate on a personal level—those that spark excitement and curiosity. These goals, however, must be grounded in realism. It's essential to consider factors such as budget constraints, health concerns, and accessibility when planning trips. Distinguishing between short local excursions and long-duration travels can help create a structured timeline of adventures, making the most out of each sojourn.

Speaking of budget, financing travel during retirement merits a careful approach. Estimating expenses isn't just about counting the cost of flights and hotels; it accounts for meals, sightseeing, souvenirs, insurance, and unforeseen costs. Forging a comprehensive budget that encapsulates all these factors is crucial to maintaining financial health while indulging in wanderlust. There are numerous ways to stretch the travel dollar—scouting for off-season deals, capitalizing on senior discounts, considering alternative lodgings like vacation rentals or hostels for a local experience, or even exploring the sharing economy for transportation and tours.

An often overlooked aspect of travel budgeting is managing money while on the move. It's wise to acquaint oneself with the nuances of currency exchange rates, international transaction fees, and safe practices for carrying money abroad. Additionally, embracing technology can facilitate smoother financial transactions and provide a sense of security: mobile banking apps keep track of spending, while digital wallets offer convenient payment options without the need to carry large amounts of cash.

While exploring the world solo has its charms, travel can also be about camaraderie and shared experiences. Retirement doesn't have to be an isolating journey. Many retirees discover a strong sense of community with individuals who share similar passions for travel. Joining clubs and groups specifically tailored for senior travelers can provide not only companionship but also valuable insights and advice. Online forums and social networks are a treasure trove of recommendations, hacks, and experiences that can enhance one's own travel plans. Furthermore, these communities often serve as support systems, offering reassurance and assistance when navigating the uncertainties associated with travel.

Building this network of travel enthusiasts also presents the opportunity to find companions for trips, making experiences more enjoyable and often more cost-effective. Beyond the practical benefits, there's an immeasurable pleasure in exchanging stories, creating shared memories, and forging lasting friendships with people from all walks of life.

The Freedom to Explore

Retirement marks a significant transition in life—a time where the conventional structure of the nine-to-five routine gives way to a period defined by the freedom to pursue personal interests and adventures at one's own pace. As retirement approaches, you find yourself at the threshold of a new chapter characterized by flexibility and the liberty to explore, both geographically and within the realms of your passions.

The concept of "time affluence," a term associated with the leisurely riches of retirement, highlights the abundance of hours available to you, unbound by the demands of a work-centric schedule. This newfound wealth of time enables you to indulge in spontaneous excursions, whether they are day trips to nearby destinations or extended travel to far-flung locales. With time as a generous companion, you can savor experiences without the rush, allowing for leisurely mornings, impromptu decisions, and the capacity to immerse fully in the present moment.

The backdrop for this freedom is the demographic shift known as the "Age Wave," where a significant portion of the population is entering retirement age, accompanied by increased life expectancy. This growing group of retirees is reshaping the landscape of leisure in their golden years. No longer seen as a period of winding down, retirement is increasingly viewed as an opportunity for new beginnings, self-discovery, and the pursuit of joy.

The flexibility during retirement extends beyond travel. It includes a broad spectrum of activities that align with personal interests and passions that may have taken a backseat during years of career focus. You can now delve into hobbies, educational pursuits, and creative projects without the constraint of time. Whether it's learning to paint, joining a dance class, or writing a memoir, the freedom of retirement allows for these engagements to flourish.

This flexibility also facilitates social connections, with you having the latitude to spend quality time with family and friends. It presents opportunities to strengthen bonds and create lasting memories through shared experiences, be it regular gatherings, vacations, or simple moments together.

Furthermore, the freedom of retirement means the ability to embrace new challenges and experiences. You can challenge yourself with goals that matter to you personally, whether it's running a marathon, volunteering for a cause you're passionate about, or engaging in lifelong learning.

Retirement leisure contributes to overall well-being and a sense of purpose during a stage of life when one's identity is often in flux. It is a time when experiences trump material possessions, and the allure of exploring, learning, and connecting takes center stage.

Planning for retirement leisure is crucial to making the most of this freedom. Considering factors such as interests, travel style, health, and budget ensures that you can tailor their explorations and experiences to their unique preferences and circumstances.

Overcoming Common Barriers to Travel

As you near retirement, a new chapter begins, filled with the promise of freedom and opportunities. The daily demands of work and time constraints start to fade, giving you more control over your time. Retirement offers a chance to step away from the structured workweek, allowing you to focus on personal enjoyment and exploration.

To make the most of this freedom, it's important to adjust your lifestyle and priorities. Whether it's taking trips you've always dreamed of, experiencing new cultures, or simply enjoying the freedom to travel whenever you choose, retirement gives you the perfect opportunity to pursue these experiences.

With careful planning and an open mind, travel can become a rewarding part of your retirement years. The world is full of places to explore, and retirement gives you the time to do it at your own pace, without work schedules holding you back. Let's delve deeper into strategies to make the most of this new phase of life, addressing the transition into a world replete with travel opportunities.

Strategic Use of Leisure Time

As discussed before, retirement gives you an abundance of what we can call 'time affluence,' one of the most significant shifts from your working life. Suddenly, you have the luxury to bask in the hours and days previously filled with professional responsibilities. Use this time wisely by identifying travel goals that speak to your passions—whether that's historical landmarks, natural wonders, culinary explorations, or arts and culture.

Prioritizing Travel

Consider making travel a top priority on your list of activities. It's tempting to fill your days with home projects or local commitments, but allowing travel to take center stage can lead to life-enriching experiences. Schedule trips as you would important appointments, ensuring they're a fixture in your calendar rather than an afterthought.

Flexibility in Planning

One tremendous benefit of retirement travel is the flexibility it offers. Without the need to coordinate with a full-time job, you can travel off-peak seasons to take advantage of fewer crowds and more affordable rates. This flexibility also means you can take advantage of last-minute deals or extend your stay at a destination that captures your heart.

Health and Mobility Considerations

Being realistic about your health and physical capabilities is paramount. There's no need to summit Everest (unless you want to!) to have a fulfilling travel experience. Plenty of destinations and activities are accessible and can be tailored to your comfort level. Always consult with a healthcare provider before embarking on strenuous trips, and consider purchasing travel insurance that covers any pre-existing conditions.

Budgeting for Travel

Transitioning to a fixed income in retirement requires careful financial planning that includes your travel aspirations. Look into destinations where the cost of living is lower, and your retirement savings will stretch further. Also, don't overlook travel discounts available for seniors—everything from flights to accommodations to entrance fees at attractions.

Travel Companions

The joy of travel is often magnified by sharing experiences with others. In retirement, you may choose to journey with a spouse or friends or join a group of like-minded travelers. Alternatively, solo travel can offer profound personal growth and the chance to meet new people.

Embrace Local and Regional Travel

Exotic destinations may be alluring, but local and regional travel can be equally fulfilling. Discovering the gems in your backyard can be done without the complexities of international travel—no currency exchange, language barriers, or lengthy flights. Short road trips, national parks, and even neighboring towns hold the potential for adventure.

Educate Yourself Through Travel

Traveling stokes the fires of learning. Engage with local cultures, take part in workshops, or enroll in short courses that allow you to dive deep into a region's history, cuisine, or art. Many educational institutions offer programs specifically designed for retirees that combine learning with travel.

Connecting With Other Travel Enthusiasts

Link up with communities, either online or in-person, that focus on retiree travel. This engagement can provide valuable tips, travel companions, and perhaps most importantly, inspiration from others who have embraced travel in their retirement.

Volunteering Abroad

Combining travel with volunteering can imbue your journeys with purpose and contribution. Many organizations welcome the skills and life experience that retirees bring to community projects around the world. You can find opportunities that range from a few weeks to several months, allowing you to make a meaningful impact while experiencing new cultures.

Stay Informed

Continually educating yourself about potential destinations is crucial. This means understanding the political climate, health risks, and any travel advisories. Keep abreast of current events in countries on your travel list and make informed decisions to ensure your safety and well-being.

Leverage Technology

Technology can be a powerful tool in planning and enjoying your travel. Apps can help you manage itineraries, handle language barriers, and even find the best local dining spots. Online platforms can also connect you with local hosts who offer a more personalized travel experience.

The Psychological Shift

The transition from a life of full-time employment to retirement is a significant psychological shift for people as they move from an environment characterized by structured workdays and responsibilities to one with unbounded free time. This change requires navigating a new landscape of self-identity and daily routine, which can be both freeing and disorienting.

For many years, the work environment has provided a natural framework for our days. Set schedules, deadlines, and tasks impose a rhythm to our lives, often dictating when we wake, eat, socialize, and rest. Work also offers a sense of purpose and achievement as we strive toward professional goals and contribute to a larger enterprise. Colleagues become a part of our social circle, and our roles within our jobs form an integral part of our identity.

Upon entering retirement, this framework dissipates. The alarm clock loses its authority, the calendar becomes less crowded, and the immediate sense of being part of a team fades. There is now a vast expanse of free time to manage without the external structure provided by a job. This can feel like a relief initially, offering an escape from the strains of work and the opportunity to engage in leisure activities without restriction.

However, the absence of an imposed routine can lead to uncertainty. Retirees may struggle to fill their days meaningfully, leading to feelings of aimlessness or boredom. Some might experience a drop in self-esteem as their professional identities recede, leaving them to ponder their purpose and value without career achievements.

Moreover, the sudden switch to a lifestyle with wide-open space for personal choice requires a recalibration of daily life. Without the need to accommodate work hours, retirees must now decide when to engage in social activities, pursue hobbies, or simply rest. The choices are endless, but making these decisions can be unexpectedly challenging.

To adapt successfully, retirees often find it essential to create a new daily routine that incorporates activities, providing a sense of fulfillment and structure. This routine might include regular physical exercise, which maintains health and introduces a stable element to the day. Volunteering or part-time work can offer opportunities to feel productive and connected. Hobbies and lifelong learning become ways to engage the mind and express creativity.

Setting Travel Goals

Setting travel goals after retirement involves choosing places and activities that stir excitement and interest. Retirement is the time to think about the locales you've always wanted to visit and the experiences you've wished to have. Identifying travel destinations and experiences you've longed for can be one of the most delightful aspects of retirement planning. It's about selecting those places that have captured your imagination through books, movies, or tales from friends and family. Your bucket list should reflect your personal dreams and aspirations as you enter this phase of freedom and discovery.

Personal interests should be the heart of your destination choices. If you're fascinated by art and history, you might be drawn to cities rich in museums and historical sites like Paris or Istanbul. Maybe you're a nature enthusiast eager to explore trails and wildlife, drawing you towards national parks or the serene countryside of destinations like New Zealand or the fjords of Norway.

When considering bucket list activities, your goals could be as adventurous as skydiving in New Zealand or as serene as taking a river cruise through the heart of Europe. Have you ever wanted to learn the tango in Argentina? Or maybe you'd like to improve your culinary skills in Italy? Now's the time to think of integrating these experiences into your travels.

Physical ability and accessibility are critical when choosing your destinations. Be honest about what level of activity you're comfortable with, as this will shape the kind of trips you plan. Countries with excellent healthcare and easy transport should be high on your list if access and medical needs are a concern.

The cultural environment of a potential destination can greatly enhance your travel experience. Consider what type of culture you're drawn to—do you seek destinations known for their friendly residents, or are those with a rich artistic heritage more your style? Maybe you want to be in a place where a particular language is spoken, allowing you to immerse yourself and practice speaking it daily.

Weather preferences also play a significant role in the enjoyment of your trips. Do you seek a warm, tropical climate to escape the colder seasons at home? Or do you prefer the cooler climates of mountainous regions? Think about the seasonal variations of your chosen destinations and plan your trip timing accordingly.

Setting a Travel Budget for Retirement

Setting a travel budget for retirement is a critical step in ensuring that you can explore new destinations without compromising your financial security. A carefully structured budget acts as a roadmap that guides your spending, allowing for a fulfilling post-retirement life filled with the joys of travel.

Examine Financial Resources

Reviewing your retirement income is like taking stock of your travel fund. Consider consistent income streams you can count on, such as retirement account distributions, pension payouts, social security benefits, or any other investments that yield regular returns. You can easily carve out a realistic sum specifically dedicated to travel by determining your monthly or annual income. It's wise not to overlook other necessary expenses, ensuring that your travel spending is a balanced portion of your overall financial plan.

Plan Detailed Expenses

Accurate estimations will safeguard against future financial stress during your travels. Start by researching the cost of airfare, which can vary widely depending on the destination and time of year. Explore different lodging options, from hotels to vacation rentals, and factor in costs for each night's stay. Don't forget ground transportation—whether you'll need rental cars, train tickets, or local transit fares. Meals are another daily expense; you might dine out frequently or occasionally cook if your accommodations allow. Every tour, museum ticket, and even the tips you give contribute to your travel expenses. Also, consider the exchange rates if you're traveling abroad; they can significantly impact your spending power.

Set Aside Funds for Unexpected Costs

Your budget should include a safety net for those times when surprises arise. Think about medical emergencies that may require visits to clinics abroad or even medical evacuation, which can be incredibly costly without proper insurance. Include a buffer for when activities are pricier than anticipated or you decide on an unplanned excursion that's too good to pass up. This fund is also useful if you encounter any travel snags like lost luggage or the need for last-minute accommodations due to a delayed flight.

Keep Track of Spending

Much like keeping a diary, maintaining a record of your expenses as you travel helps you stay accountable and financially on track. Use tools like budgeting apps, spreadsheets, or even a simple notebook to log every purchase and compare it against your planned budget. If you notice you're consistently overspending in an area, such as dining, make adjustments to other parts of your budget to compensate. Regularly checking in on your spending helps you stay flexible and make financial decisions that align with your priorities.

Balancing Travel Dreams With Practical Considerations

Setting travel goals after retirement requires careful consideration of both your dreams and practical realities like budget constraints and health issues. Striking the right balance can be challenging, but with the right approach, you can ensure that your travels are both achievable and enjoyable. Your retirement years offer a unique opportunity to fulfill your travel dreams. This is the time you've envisioned exploring new cultures, soaking in diverse landscapes, and experiencing the wonders of the world. While dreaming big is encouraged, it's equally important to approach your travel plans practically.

As discussed earlier, the budget is one of the core factors to consider. Start by reviewing your financial health. Determine what portion of your savings or income can be allocated to travel without compromising your essential expenses. Creating a budget for your travel plans gives you a clearer picture of what you can afford and helps prevent overspending. It's a step that also adds a layer of security, ensuring that your finances remain stable throughout your retirement.

Equally crucial is considering your health when planning your getaways. Health issues can arise unexpectedly, and certain destinations might be more challenging to navigate if you're dealing with mobility limitations or other medical conditions. It's wise to discuss your travel plans with a healthcare provider, ensuring that you have the necessary medications and are clear on any preventive measures, such as vaccinations or health insurance, that align with your destinations' requirements.

Creating a Travel Timeline

When envisioning your retirement travels, think about creating a timeline that alternates between short getaways and more extended vacations. Short trips can provide a refreshing break from routine and often require less planning and budgeting. These can include weekend stays at a beach resort, visits to nearby cities, or short cruises. They offer the benefits of relaxation and a change of scenery without the need for extensive preparation.

Extended trips, on the other hand, allow for immersion into new environments, cultures, and experiences. They are the perfect opportunity to tick off those once-in-a-lifetime destinations from your bucket list. Planning for longer trips demands more attention to details such as the best time of year to visit, booking arrangements, and packing adequately for the duration of your stay.

When planning these longer stints, consider travel during the off-season when prices are generally lower and tourist spots are less crowded. You have the flexibility to enjoy locations at a leisurely pace, which in turn could positively benefit your budget.

In both cases, advance planning is key to stress-free travel. For short getaways, you might focus on taking advantage of last-minute deals. For extended travels, you might plan months in advance, which could yield early booking discounts or ample time to plan for cost-effective routes and accommodations.

Budgeting for Travel

Creating a budget for travel after retirement is essential to ensure that your adventures are both enjoyable and financially sustainable. The excitement of exploring new places should be matched with a clear plan for managing expenses. Let's explore how you can estimate and manage your travel expenses effectively.

Estimating Travel Costs

When it comes to estimating travel costs for your retirement adventures, a detailed approach can help you prepare a realistic and effective budget. By considering various elements that contribute to your trip expenses, you'll be better equipped to enjoy your travels without worry.

Destination Research

The first step in your planning should be to thoroughly research your chosen destinations. The cost of living varies widely from one country to another and even within regions of the same country. Websites like Numbeo, as well as travel blogs and forums, can provide insights into the average costs for accommodations, dining, and popular tourist activities. Remember to look into the seasonal price fluctuations that may affect your budget.

Travel Style

Your personal travel style significantly influences your budget. If you prefer luxury hotels and fine dining, your daily expenditures will be higher than if you're comfortable with guesthouses and street food. Consider whether you'll need a rental car, whether you'll be taking public transport, or if you're planning to walk or bike most of the time. These choices impact the cost as well as the kind of experiences you'll have.

Factor in All Travel Expenses

A comprehensive travel budget includes all potential expenditures. Start with the major costs, like flights or other transportation to and from your destination. Then factor in accommodation choices, whether you'll be staying in hotels, bed-and-breakfasts, or renting through services like Airbnb. Consider ancillary costs, like luggage fees, travel insurance, and airport shuttles. Think about daily meals, funds for sightseeing and guided tours, entry fees to attractions, and the occasional splurge on something special like a show or a fancy dinner. Lastly, a little extra for souvenirs or local markets can ensure you have a token to remember your travels by.

Create a Travel Budget

Armed with the information from your research, draft a travel budget that covers all aspects of your trip. Use a spreadsheet to track all possible costs, allocating a section for each category of spending. This could include transportation, lodging, meals, activities, shopping, and miscellaneous expenses. Be sure to add a buffer of around 10-20% of the total budget for unexpected costs, like a medical emergency, last-minute itinerary changes, or even minor things like tips or a snack at a rest stop.

Strategies for Saving Money on Travel

Traveling does not have to break the bank. By implementing a few strategic cost-saving methods, retirees can stretch their travel dollars further. Let's delve into more detailed strategies to keep your travel expenses in check:

Keep an eye out for special promotion periods, and limited-time offers that could significantly slash prices. Join forums and groups dedicated to retiree travel where members often share exclusive deals or group discount opportunities.

Visiting destinations outside of peak tourist seasons can result in drastic savings on accommodation and activities. For instance, visiting Europe during fall or winter—outside of the Christmas season—can lead to lower airfare and hotel costs compared to the summer months.

Venturing beyond traditional hotels can provide not only savings but also a more authentic travel experience. Vacation rentals through platforms like Airbnb often offer better value, particularly for longer stays. They come with added benefits, like kitchens that enable home cooking, washing facilities, and more space. For a community-oriented experience, consider homestays or hostels, and don't overlook services that allow for longer-term stays in exchange for house-sitting or pet-sitting.

Staying loyal to certain travel brands through their rewards programs can lead to free or discounted flights, stays, and upgrades. Credit cards that specialize in travel rewards can also be an effective way to earn points on everyday purchases that you can redeem for travel expenses.

Managing Finances While Traveling

Good financial management while traveling can prevent unpleasant surprises and ensure your retirement savings are not unduly depleted. Here are some more detailed tips for controlling your spending while indulging your love for travel:

Technology today offers many apps that can help with budgeting; you can track what you're spending in real-time and categorize your expenses. This approach provides clear visibility over your finances so you can adjust your spending as needed.

When you're in a different country, using local currency is usually more cost-effective. Avoid currency exchange services at airports and hotels where rates are less favorable. Using a credit card without international fees or withdrawing money from ATMs in larger amounts to reduce transaction fees is typically more economical.

To enjoy local cuisine without the restaurant price tag, mix dining out with self-catering. Visit local supermarkets and prepare some meals at your accommodation. When you do eat out, consider lunch specials, which are often less expensive than dinner menus.

Many destinations offer enriching experiences that are completely free. You might enjoy historical walks, visit free museums or galleries, relax in public parks, hike in nature reserves, or attend local cultural events and markets. Research ahead and plan your itinerary to include these complimentary attractions.

To avoid blowing your budget on any given day, set a daily spending limit and stick to it. Money saved on a day can be rolled over, allowing you to splurge on a special occasion without guilt. Always keep track of your finances so you know where your money is going.

Connectivity can be costly, especially with international roaming. Buying a local SIM card for data and calls can be much cheaper than roaming charges. Alternatively, take advantage of free Wi-Fi in hotels, cafes, and public spaces, but always ensure a secure connection when accessing personal and financial information.

Building a Travel Community

Building a travel community as a retiree opens up a new world of possibilities and connections. When you retire, suddenly, there's time to explore destinations at your own pace, immerse yourself in new cultures, and create memories to last a lifetime. Connecting with other retirees who share your passion for travel can enhance this chapter in your life by providing companionship, advice, and shared experiences.

Many retirees find value in joining travel clubs and groups, which offer not just opportunities for group travel but also workshops, social gatherings, and an instant network of friendship and support. These clubs often cater to a wide range of interests and can provide valuable information on everything from snatching up the best travel deals to preparing for international adventures.

Participating in travel clubs and groups offers numerous benefits. You get the chance to meet people who are also exploring what it means to travel during this stage of life. Their insights and first-hand experiences can be invaluable whether you're seeking travel hacks or recommendations for the best places to visit. Plus, they understand the nuances of traveling as a retiree, from the complexity of health considerations to the joy of having no set timetable.

In addition to physical meetups, online forums offer a space for travelers to connect virtually. These forums often have subgroups dedicated to cruising, solo travel, budget travel, and more. Online communities are a treasure trove of knowledge, brimming with trip reports, destination advice, safety tips, and packing lists that other community members have shared. They can be easy to navigate and a springboard to forging new friendships.

Social networks can be another resource for finding travel partners and sharing experiences. Platforms like Facebook have groups where you can post travel photos, seek advice, or simply chat about upcoming plans. Twitter and Instagram can be good for real-time updates and connecting with fellow travelers, while Pinterest might inspire your next trip with picturesque images and blog posts.

Sharing your travel experiences on these networks can be as rewarding as the travel itself. You can write about your adventures, share photos, and participate in discussions about your encounters. Others in your community may comment, offer encouragement, or suggest new ideas for your next trip.

In this social sphere, you might find others who are planning trips to places you've never considered but now wish to explore. And sometimes, you'll run into like-minded companions who are looking to travel but not alone. This can lead to forming new friendships with travel companions who share your wanderlust and zest for new adventures.

Retirement ushers in an era of unprecedented freedom, allowing retirees to finally enjoy the pleasures and adventures they've postponed while working. It's a time to embrace new hobbies, gather unique experiences, and connect with others who share the same zest for life. While setting travel plans in motion, it becomes crucial to pair aspirations with practical considerations, maintain financial well-being, and adapt to the psychological transition from career to leisure. Whether it's delving into long-awaited trips, exploring the world, or simply savoring the pleasures of a flexible schedule, retirement indeed presents a remarkable opportunity for personal growth and enjoyment. With prudent planning, this stage of life can be as exciting and fulfilling as one chooses it to be, proving that the golden years can truly glitter with the promise of new discoveries and cherished experiences.

Chapter 2:

The Pension Fund Is Ready—

It's Time to Start Using It!

Reaching the point where your pension fund is ready to support you is a major milestone in life. It marks the beginning of a new chapter, where the hard work and savings of your career can finally provide you with the financial security and comfort you deserve. However, transitioning into this phase requires careful planning and thoughtful decisions.—

Now is the time to think about how you'll start using the funds you've accumulated over the years. Every dollar should be used wisely to ensure it not only meets your current needs but also supports you for the long haul. It's crucial to take a step back and assess your financial situation, considering not just your pension but any other income sources you might have. This could include Social Security, personal savings, or investments you've made along the way.

Another key aspect of this stage is figuring out how best to withdraw from your pension. Should you take a lump sum all at once, or would systematic withdrawals over time give you more stability? The choices you make here will shape your financial flexibility and security in the years to come. Balancing these decisions with tax planning and investment strategies will help minimize unnecessary costs and allow your savings to work more efficiently for you.

When you step into retirement, your healthcare needs and estate planning also become more important. Preparing for medical expenses and ensuring your estate plans are up to date will give you peace of mind and help preserve your legacy.

Evaluating Your Financial Landscape

When considering your financial future, especially as retirement approaches, an essential step is to take a close look at your pension fund. A pension can be a significant source of income during your retirement years, so it's well worth your time to get to grips with what type of pension plan you have and the specifics of your plan.

Assessing Your Pension Fund

First, determine the type of pension plan you have. There are mainly two kinds: defined benefit and defined contribution plans. A defined benefit plan is the more traditional option, where you receive a fixed income in retirement, which is calculated based on your salary and years of service. In contrast, a defined contribution plan, such as a 401(k), relics on the contributions you and possibly your employer have made, as well as the performance of the investments over time. The payout from this type of plan is not guaranteed, as it will depend on the balance in your account at the time you retire (Rosentson, 2024).

Now, let's address understanding your specific pension plan in more detail:

Learn What Type of Pension Plan You Have

Start by gathering all the documentation related to your pension. That might be summary plan descriptions, annual statements, or benefit illustrations. Identify who administers your plan—it might be your employer, a pension fund, or an insurance company. You should also find out whether your pension is covered by the Pension Benefit Guaranty Corporation (PBGC), a US government agency that protects pension benefits in private-sector defined-benefit plans (Rosentson, 2024).

For a defined-benefit plan, look at the formula that will determine your retirement payouts. Typically, this formula is based on your salary and years of service. For example, your plan might offer 1.5% of your average salary for the last five years of your employment, multiplied by the total number of years you worked for the company (Rosentson, 2024).

If you have a defined contribution plan, check your current balance and understand how that money is invested. Are you in stocks, bonds, mutual funds, or a mix? What are the expected returns on those investments? What fees are you paying? All these factors will impact your balance over time.

Next, you should determine when you can access your pension funds. For many plans, you can start receiving benefits at the "normal retirement age," which often is 65. However, there might be options for early retirement or deferred retirement, which could increase or decrease your payments.

Understanding Your Specific Plan Details (e.g., Payout Options, Terms)

Once you have a handle on the type of plan you're enrolled in, drill down into the nitty-gritty. There are various payout options to consider, especially for a defined-benefit plan. You might have the choice between a lump-sum payout, where you receive the entire value of your pension in one go, or annuity payments, which provide a steady income stream for life or a set period. Each has advantages and disadvantages, depending on your personal circumstances and financial goals.

If you're married, consider benefits for your spouse. Many pension plans offer survivor benefits, ensuring that your spouse continues to receive a payout after your death. The specifics, however, can vary widely, so get familiar with your plan's provisions. Some plans reduce the payout if you opt for a joint-and-survivor annuity.

Don't overlook the inflation protection feature. Some pensions include cost-of-living adjustments (COLAs), which increase your payments over time to keep up with inflation. Your plan documents should detail how COLAs are calculated and when they are applied.

Another key factor in understanding your pension plan is vesting. Vesting refers to the period of time you must work for your employer before you become entitled to all or a portion of your pension benefits. If you leave your job before you are fully vested, you could lose some or even all of the benefits you've accumulated.

Evaluate other benefits that your pension plan might offer, too, such as early retirement options or disability benefits. There may be criteria to meet for these benefits, like age and years of service requirements or specific medical qualifications. Also, review your plan's statement for unclaimed benefits. Sometimes, especially in the case of people who move jobs frequently, pension benefits might go unclaimed.

Finally, it's wise to keep an eye on the financial health of your pension plan. The funded status of a pension plan—how well the plan's assets cover its obligations—is a strong indicator of its stability. If a defined-benefit plan isn't well-funded, it could mean that the company might not be able to honor its commitments in the future.

Take the time to fully investigate your pension fund. Understand whether it's a defined-benefit or defined-contribution plan, the details of your payout options, and the terms of the plan. Doing this work upfront will help you plan more effectively for a financially secure retirement. Staying educated about your pension plan is crucial, as it may change over time due to alterations in government regulations or company policies. So, keep updated with the latest plan documents, and don't hesitate to reach out to your plan administrator with any questions or concerns you might have. Your future self will thank you for taking charge of your retirement well-being.

Analyzing Additional Income Sources

When you're looking ahead to days filled with more freedom and perhaps fewer work responsibilities, counting all possible income sources becomes vital. For many, that future financial landscape includes Social Security, personal savings, various investments, and, on occasion, additional cash flow from part-time work or rental income. Let's discuss how you can examine these streams and ensure they align with your vision for retirement.

Social Security

For most of us, Social Security is a cornerstone of retirement income. The system was set up to supplement your golden years, though it was never intended to be the sole source of post-career sustenance. Despite its reliability, it's worth noting that your lifestyle in retirement shouldn't lean entirely on these benefits.

To maximize the income from Social Security, a measured approach to when you begin your benefits is critical. Generally, the rule is simple: the earlier you start, the smaller the checks; the longer you defer up to age 70, the heftier the monthly amount becomes. Decisions around when you claim Social Security should be synchronized with your overall financial situation, health, and life expectancy. If you're in great shape and longevity runs in the family, waiting a bit longer before tapping into Social Security makes sense as the increments increase your payouts.

Evaluating your benefits can't start early enough. If you're over 60, you should receive statements by mail, but these documents, along with estimates for various retirement ages, are accessible anytime online at the Social Security Administration's website. It's prudent to periodically log into your My Social Security account to verify the accuracy of your earnings history and get updated estimates of your benefit amounts.

The formula for calculating your benefit is somewhat complicated, but it essentially uses your 35 highest-earning years, adjusted for inflation, to determine your monthly amount. It behooves you to ensure that your earning records are accurate and that any higher earning years haven't been mistakenly omitted.

Personal Savings

Contrasting with the somewhat passive nature of Social Security, your personal savings reflect proactive efforts and financial discipline over many years. Whether it's money set aside in a high-yield savings account, a traditional IRA, a Roth IRA, a 401(k), or other retirement vehicles, personal savings can greatly influence the quality and comfort of your retirement life. These accounts are particularly important because they offer ways to save with tax advantages, either now or in the future.

The 401(k) stands out as a staple in many retirement portfolios, especially beneficial for its higher contribution limits and potential employer matching programs. The compound interest and tax deferral on growth it offers can significantly bolster your retirement fund. Evaluating the mix of investment options within your 401(k), like stock funds for growth and bond funds for stability, and aligning them with your risk tolerance is a key strategy leading up to and into retirement.

IRAs, conversely, offer a bit more flexibility in investment choices, and deciding between a traditional IRA, which offers a tax deduction now, and a Roth IRA, which promises tax-free withdrawals later, usually depends on your current and expected future tax brackets. The traditional IRA may suit those anticipating a lower tax rate in retirement, while the Roth IRA might benefit those expecting higher tax rates later.

It's vital to look at the sum total of these accounts regularly and make proactive decisions about contributions, investment choices, and potential rollovers. For example, if a career change occurs, what will you do with your 401(k)? Will you roll it over into an IRA or leave it with your former employer's plan?

Each of these choices will leave different marks on your savings landscape. Understanding the nuances of each account, from early withdrawal penalties to required minimum distributions, will help you navigate the retirement terrain without unnecessary financial sacrifice.

In both cases—Social Security and personal savings—the trick to having enough in retirement is to be proactive, well-informed, and strategic. Leveraging these tools to your advantage can spell the difference between merely getting by in retirement and thriving through your senior years.

Creating a Diverse Investment Garden

A diverse investment portfolio may include a mix of stocks, bonds, mutual funds, ETFs, and other financial instruments, including potentially valuable real estate holdings. Diversifying is fundamental because not all investments flourish simultaneously; while one might be experiencing growth, another might face a decline. Think of it as not putting all your apples in one basket, so if one basket drops, you still have plenty of apples left.

Bonds

Bonds, for instance, are like the slow-growers. They're the stalwart trees that may not tower swiftly, but over time, they provide consistent yields. They're typically more stable and less volatile, and they pay out interest at regular intervals, which can be re-invested or used as a steady source of income.

Stocks

Stocks are generally the more vibrant flowers in your garden. They can surge, adding bursts of color and value to your portfolio, or they can wilt, detracting from your garden's overall health. Stocks that pay dividends can be especially appealing because they offer a steady income, which can be beneficial when other parts of your investment portfolio aren't performing as well.

Mutual Funds and ETFs

Mutual funds and ETFs are like mixed flower beds. They offer an assortment of various stocks, bonds, or other assets managed by financial experts. These funds allow you to own a small portion of multiple investments without the need to manage each one individually. They are an excellent way to achieve diversification and can be selected based on the level of risk you're comfortable with.

Real Estate

And then there's real estate. A well-located property can appreciate significantly over time, and it can often provide rental income, which can make a big difference in retirement. But remember, real estate is not as liquid as stocks or bonds—it can take time to sell if you need access to your investment quickly.

Assessing Your Investment Health

When retirement nears, it becomes crucial to assess the health of these investments. What's the risk factor of your portfolio? Does it align with your decreasing appetite for risk as you age? It might be time to talk with a financial planner about shifting gears, moving from aggressive or moderate-aggressive investment strategies to more moderate or conservative approaches. This doesn't mean you stop growing your investment garden; you're just switching to nurturing a more resilient, perhaps slightly less bountiful patch.

Part-Time Work

With your investment portfolio strategically aligned with your upcoming retirement needs, let's focus on another stream that can keep your financial engine humming smoothly: part-time work.

The decision to continue working after retirement often isn't solely about money, though that's an obvious perk. Part-time work can bring joy, provide social interaction, and offer a sense of purpose. Whether it's consulting in your seasoned profession or something entirely new and passion-driven, part-time work can ease the transition from a full-time career to a fully retired life.

From a fiscal standpoint, part-time employment allows for financial flexibility. It means there's less need to withdraw from your investment portfolio, giving it more breathing room to grow or at least maintain its health. In essence, you're adding a splash of water to your investment garden during retirement's summer months, ensuring the plants there remain vibrant.

The strategic value of part-time income in retirement can't be overstated. It can also equate to delaying Social Security benefits, allowing your future benefits to increase by about 8% for each year you delay, up until age 70.

Finding the Right Fit

What's essential in finding part-time work is balancing the joy it brings against its demand on your time. Does it offer the flexibility you desire? Are the hours and workload manageable and not overriding the reason you stepped away from a career? Seek out roles that fit the lifestyle you envision for your later years. Always keep in mind that part-time work is not just about padding your finances. It's more about maintaining your identity, your engagement with the world, and shaping your daily life in a way that brings you happiness.

Part-time work might involve becoming an entrepreneur—turning a hobby into a business or offering your expertise as an independent consultant. It's contributing without the stress of full-time work, providing service in a way that acknowledges your expertise and respects your time.

Engage Without Overcommitting

As you think about adding part-time work to your retirement plan, the key is to engage without overcommitting. The luster of extra income should not outshine your need for personal time, relaxation, and the pursuit of hobbies and interests. Find a happy equilibrium.

Integrating a diligent investment strategy alongside the option for part-time work can amplify your financial security blanket in retirement. It's embracing work that adds value to your life without burdening your freedom. Both strategies require a thoughtful approach—a balancing act of foresight, planning, and a touch of daring.

So, how do you put this puzzle together? Start by listing all your income sources with their expected values after you retire. Next, line these up against your anticipated expenses. If you're spreadsheet-savvy, plugging in these figures can help you visualize where you stand. There are plenty of online tools to help as well, some catered specifically to retirement planning.

Things like healthcare costs, inflation, and your own longevity are also factors in this matrix. The costs of daily living won't freeze just because you stop working. And, statistically speaking, we're living longer, so your funds need a longer runway than they might have in the past. Bringing in help from a financial advisor could be a wise move, too. They can help create a more precise picture and advise on any adjustments to your savings or investment strategies.

Planning for retirement doesn't stop at expecting Social Security checks or eyeing your savings account balance. It's about actively taking the reins on various income sources. Include part-time work or rental income if it suits your lifestyle and adds to your sense of purpose.

A successful retirement is a blend of careful finance and personal happiness. By calculating and arranging your resources thoughtfully, you create a solid foundation that frees you to relish the adventures of your later years without financial stress shadowing your every step.

Crafting a Sustainable Withdrawal Strategy

Crafting a sustainable withdrawal strategy is a significant component of financial planning, particularly for those transitioning into retirement. The decision between taking lump sum withdrawals versus periodic withdrawals is a critical one, with implications for your long-term financial stability and flexibility. Let's explore the pros and cons of both approaches and how they might affect your financial future.

Lump Sum Withdrawals

Lump sum withdrawals can be quite a tempting option when you reach retirement. Think of it like holding a full basket of apples all at once. It feels substantial, and it's yours to do with as you please. You might have a long-awaited dream you want to fund, like buying an RV and touring the country or perhaps renovating your home to host family gatherings.

When you opt for a lump sum, the immediate access to funds definitely has its perks. Paying off a lingering mortgage or clearing credit card debts can be a huge relief. Maybe you've been eyeing an investment such as real estate that could bring more income. Such control can be liberating since you decide how to use, invest, or save these funds. But it's not all sunshine. Major financial decisions often come with complex tax implications. Taking your retirement savings in one go could bump you up to a higher tax bracket, much like moving into a bigger house might increase your property taxes. This means your nest egg is immediately diminished by a significant tax bite.

Now, consider what happens if you spend too much too soon. You could face the reality of your financial wellspring drying up. This is particularly concerning if you expect to have a long retirement.

Your lump sum could have grown if it was invested over time. Withdrawing it all means you miss out on potential investment returns—the financial fruits you could have enjoyed had you left your apples to grow into an orchard over time.

Emotionally, having a lot of money at hand can lead to splurging—suddenly, every upgrade seems necessary, and indulgences become harder to resist. It's crucial to think about whether you can manage such a sum without the temptation to overspend, affecting your judgment.

Periodic Withdrawals

Shifting gears, let's talk about the systematic approach—periodic withdrawals. It's almost like receiving a paycheck, providing you with a steady stream of income. This can make transitions into retirement smoother since your financial life continues to have a familiar rhythm.

The beauty of spreading out your withdrawals is that it often lowers your yearly tax bill because you're not taking out as much at one time. What's more, your money has the chance to grow. The part that remains invested can still appreciate, potentially outpacing inflation and preserving your purchasing power.

Consider this: avoiding the challenge of market timing. Regular withdrawals mean you sell assets over time, not all at once, which can work to your advantage if the market dips. You're not trying to pick the best time to sell everything, which even seasoned investors find tricky.

The ongoing maintenance of periodic withdrawals does add some complexity. It demands attention to your investments, choices about how much to take out, and, sometimes, a reshuffling of your financial deck. You'll need to stay reasonably informed and make periodic adjustments. If life throws you a financial curveball, your funds aren't as immediately accessible because they're programmed to be dispensed over time.

Then there's the stock market's mercurial nature. If it takes a downturn, your withdrawals could take a bigger slice of your principal than expected, which could diminish your portfolio's ability to bounce back. You have to keep an eye on market trends and portfolio performance, possibly rejiggering your approach in response to market movements.

Ultimately, periodic withdrawals might be less exciting—or intimidating—than receiving a lump sum, but they offer peace of mind. You can sleep better knowing there's a plan in place ensuring you have a predictable income throughout retirement.

Both lump sum and systematic withdrawal strategies need a plan; they're just different types of plans. If you're hands-on and eager to manage your finances closely, lump sum withdrawals offer an opportunity—mixed with responsibility. If you prefer a more hands-off approach, systematic withdrawals could provide a steady, predictable income that suits a careful, long-term strategy.

Impact on Long-term Financial Stability and Flexibility

When it comes to long-term financial stability, periodic withdrawals often come out ahead. They provide a sustainable income that can last throughout retirement, especially if structured to adjust to inflation and increase longevity. This method allows you to maintain some level of investment in the market, which could offset inflation over time.

Lump sum withdrawals, while providing immediate access and control, place the onus on you to manage that money responsibly. Without careful planning, you might outlive your savings. Moreover, the initial tax impact of a lump sum could diminish the fund's worth right from the beginning.

In terms of flexibility, lump sum withdrawals obviously give you more immediate freedom to manage your money as you like. However, that comes with greater responsibility and the need to exercise restraint to ensure that your funds last. Periodic withdrawals are less flexible initially, as you set up a schedule you need to stick to, but they offer greater peace of mind by providing a stable income for the future.

Planning for the endgame is all about balance. It's about considering what will keep you financially afloat and comfortable for the rest of your life. Will you be safer with a structured, regular income? Or do you have the financial chops to take a big pile of money and make it last, potentially growing it while living the life you've dreamed about?

The choice is personal and should reflect your life's work, your dreams, your discipline, and your peace of mind. Weigh your options, consider seeking advice from a trusted financial advisor, and tread the path that's right for you. Stay informed, stay sensible, and, above all, make sure your retirement is everything you've worked so hard for it to be.

Implementing an Effective Withdrawal Plan

Creating an effective withdrawal plan for retirement is about balancing the need for immediate income with the desire to make your savings last. Let's break it down into two distinct points: choosing the right withdrawal rate and adjusting that rate according to various factors like life expectancy and market fluctuations.

Determining the Right Withdrawal Rate

Finding a magic number that balances the risk of running out of money against the need for a comfortable lifestyle is critical. In retirement, the initial withdrawal rate is a percentage of your savings that you decide to withdraw in the first year. This is followed by annual adjustments. The 4% rule, which implies drawing down 4% of your retirement savings every year, adjusted for inflation, is a well-known starting point. However, this rate is not one-size-fits-all.

You want a strategy that keeps up with inflation and accommodates personal spending needs. Some might be able to live comfortably on a 3% withdrawal rate, while others might need 5% or higher. Here's how to personalize your withdrawal rate:

- Assess your total retirement savings and consider the types of accounts you have, such as 401(k), IRAs, and taxable accounts.
- Look at your expected expenses and any other income sources, including Social Security, pensions, or part-time work.

- Use financial calculators or work with a financial advisor to forecast how different withdrawal rates will affect the longevity of your savings.
- Review your health history and family longevity to gauge your life expectancy, which will play a role in how long your savings need to last.

Adjusting Withdrawals Based on Life Expectancy

Life is not static, and neither should your approach to retirement withdrawals. Your nest egg needs to be managed with flexibility and adaptability as you navigate the changing tides of your personal life and market fluctuations. Let's talk about adjusting for life expectancy first. This is a delicate subject, but it's also a fundamental aspect of financial planning. As years roll by, it's wise to periodically reassess your life expectancy. Advances in medicine could mean that your health outlook and longevity may surpass your initial expectations, and you need to be ready for this happy possibility. Subsequently, this could mean that a lower withdrawal rate might be more appropriate to prevent the risk of outliving your funds.

However, life expectancy is just one part of the equation. More immediate are the ever-volatile market conditions. The value of your investments can be significantly affected by economic downturns or booms. When the market looks grim and your portfolio's value dips, it makes sense to tighten the belt a little and reduce your withdrawal rate. Conversely, a flourishing market might tempt you to withdraw more, but caution is still the key. It might be wiser to recover the ground lost during the less prosperous years or to save for a rainier day.

But how do you implement these strategies wisely? First, select a reasonable start point for your withdrawals—most likely a percentage of your portfolio. This will be your baseline. But understand that this is just the beginning. Each year (or more frequently, if necessary), you'll need to gauge multiple factors:

- Have there been major changes in the cost of living, or have there been significant lifestyle changes that necessitate spending adjustments?
- How has the market's health been? Are your investments inching upward, holding steady, or facing a downturn?
- Have you encountered unexpected healthcare costs, or have you decided to splurge on new experiences?

These questions will guide your decisions. If the market's down, you may want to cut back on nonessential spending to lessen the withdrawals. It's a bit like sailing: when the waters are choppy, you reduce your sail to maintain control.

Let's suppose the market is thriving, and you've enjoyed some gains. You could be tempted to increase your withdrawal rate. It's fine to reward yourself, maybe with a trip or a generous gift for the grandchildren, but it's also prudent to consider how your actions today will affect your portfolio's longevity.

Life throws curveballs, and occasionally, they come fast and furious. In these instances, even the most conservative withdrawal schedule may need to be ramped up to deal with whatever life tosses at you, be it a leaky roof or an unforeseen medical expense. Flexibility is essential, so build a buffer into your plans for such moments.

As for the nuts and bolts of actually implementing your plan, choose a withdrawal method that syncs with how you manage your life. Some people relish the predictability of monthly disbursements; it's similar to receiving a paycheck and can make budgeting straightforward. Others might prefer quarterly or annual withdrawals, which could be tied to specific expenses or events.

In any case, keep an eye on how each withdrawal affects your overall portfolio. If a monthly withdrawal eats into your principal more than you're comfortable with, consider adjusting either the amount or the frequency. Your aim is to strike a balance between sustaining your lifestyle and sustaining your portfolio.

This is a unique journey, and so is your financial path. There's no single formula or strategy that suits everyone equally. Your plan will need reviewing, tweaking, and sometimes even overhauling, especially when faced with significant shifts in the market or life circumstances.

Visualize your retirement plan as a living thing—it grows, it changes, and it needs nurturing.

Ongoing Review and Adjustment

Avoid putting your withdrawal plan on autopilot. Make it a habit to review it annually or more often if there's a major life event or a significant shift in the market. During these reviews:

- Check your portfolio's performance against your withdrawal rate.
- Decide if you need to make any changes to your spending habits or withdrawal rate.
- Factor in any major health or lifestyle changes that have occurred or are anticipated.
- Consult with a financial professional to get a nuanced perspective or to help navigate complex scenarios.

The goal is to strike a balance between enjoying retirement and not outliving your assets. An effective withdrawal plan is flexible, prudent, and adjusts to life's rhythms. It allows for indulgences—like that dream vacation or a new car—while also preparing for the unexpected.

Good planning and regular reassessments are the cornerstones of a sustainable withdrawal strategy. With these practices, you can find peace of mind in knowing that you've taken control of your financial future in a thoughtful, strategic way.

Managing Investments and Minimizing Taxes

When planning for retirement, managing taxes is crucial to ensuring financial stability in the long run. To achieve this, you need a clear strategy that not only maximizes the growth of your assets but also minimizes the tax burden on withdrawals. Let's explore how you can adapt your investment strategy and understand the tax implications, ensuring a smoother financial journey through retirement.

Adapting Your Investment Strategy

A smart investment strategy is key to managing your assets efficiently. To craft a strategy that works for your unique situation, it is often recommended to work closely with an investment specialist. Here's why:

Collaborating With an Investment Specialist

No two retirement plans are exactly the same. An investment specialist can help you tailor a strategy that aligns with your financial goals, taking into account your risk tolerance, retirement timeline, and long-term financial needs. For instance, they can help you decide the right balance between growth and income-producing investments and determine how much of your savings should be allocated to each.

Another important aspect is that they stay updated on the latest market trends and tax regulations. This ensures that your portfolio is not only performing optimally but is also structured in a tax-efficient way. Given that tax laws change frequently, this guidance can help you stay on track and avoid any unnecessary tax penalties down the line.

Tax Implications

Taxes can have a significant impact on the money you have available during retirement. The timing and type of withdrawals you make from different accounts can result in vastly different tax outcomes. When taking money out of retirement accounts, it's crucial to be aware of the tax implications associated with each type of account. Here's a general overview:

Taxable Accounts

These accounts, like brokerage accounts, are subject to capital gains taxes on the sale of investments. Depending on how long you've held the asset, you could be taxed at a higher short-term rate or a more favorable long-term rate. If you have taxable investments, it may make sense to hold onto them for over a year to qualify for the lower long-term capital gains tax rate (Boyte-White, 2019).

Traditional Retirement Accounts (401(k), Traditional IRAs)

Withdrawals from these accounts are generally taxed as ordinary income. This means that the more you withdraw, the higher your tax bracket may be. It's important to plan withdrawals carefully to avoid being pushed into a higher tax bracket unexpectedly (Boyte-White, 2019).

Roth Accounts

The withdrawals from Roth IRAs or Roth 401(k)s are generally tax-free, provided certain conditions are met. These can be a useful tool to balance out taxable income, particularly later in retirement when your tax rate might increase (Boyte-White, 2019).

Strategies for Tax-Efficient Withdrawals

One of the complexities of retirement is the need to balance withdrawals across different types of accounts in a tax-efficient manner. A few strategies that can help include:

Spreading Out Withdrawals to Minimize Taxes

One effective method is to spread out withdrawals over time, starting with taxable accounts, followed by tax-deferred accounts, and then Roth accounts. This can help prevent you from having a large taxable income in any given year. For example, if you need to sell investments from taxable accounts, doing so earlier could help avoid large capital gains later in retirement.

Managing Required Minimum Distributions (RMDs)

Once you turn 73 (or 75 in certain cases, depending on recent changes to tax laws), you'll be required to take RMDs from traditional IRAs, 401(k)s, and other tax-deferred retirement accounts. These distributions are taxed as ordinary income and can push you into a higher tax bracket (Cheng, 2024). To avoid this, you might want to start taking smaller withdrawals before you reach the age of RMDs, spreading the tax impact over multiple years.

Proportional Withdrawals

Another strategy is proportional withdrawals, where you withdraw a percentage of your retirement income from each type of account. This method can reduce tax volatility and may help you lower your lifetime tax burden. Instead of withdrawing from one account entirely before moving on to the next, this method balances withdrawals across accounts to maintain a more consistent tax rate throughout retirement.

Consider Qualified Medical Expenses

Using tax-free accounts like a Health Savings Account (HSA) for qualified medical expenses can also be a helpful way to reduce taxable income. Withdrawals from HSAs are tax-free if used for medical expenses, which may become a more significant part of your spending in retirement.

Planning Ahead to Optimize Your Strategy

Tax planning should be ongoing, as your tax situation may change due to various factors, such as changes in the tax code, lifestyle changes (like deciding to work part-time), or even health expenses. It's essential to stay in touch with both your financial advisor and tax professional to regularly review and adjust your strategy. This ensures that your investments continue to grow while keeping your tax burden as low as possible.

Planning for Healthcare and Estate Needs

Planning for healthcare and estate needs is essential as you age. Both healthcare expenses and estate planning play a significant role in ensuring that your financial security and legacy are well-protected. In this section, we'll explore how to prepare for healthcare costs and the steps to take when updating your estate plan so you can have peace of mind in the years ahead.

Preparing for Healthcare Expenses

Healthcare expenses are one of the most significant financial concerns people face as they age. Without proper planning, medical costs can quickly spiral out of control, putting pressure on your savings. Let's explore how you can anticipate and manage these expenses effectively:

Estimating and Managing Out-of-Pocket Medical Costs

Healthcare costs in retirement extend beyond just insurance premiums. You also need to account for deductibles, co-pays, prescription drugs, and potential medical procedures. The first step in preparing for these out-of-pocket costs is to understand what you may need to spend over time.

Start by looking at your current health status and any known medical conditions. Try to estimate the type of care you may require in the future. For example, individuals with chronic conditions might need ongoing medications or therapies that could add up. It's also essential to include dental, vision, and hearing care, as these are often not covered by Medicare.

To help manage these costs, consider creating a separate budget specifically for medical expenses. This can give you a clearer picture of how much to allocate for healthcare each year. Additionally, it's wise to explore tax-advantaged savings accounts like Health Savings Accounts (HSAs) while you are still working. An HSA allows you to set aside pre-tax money to cover future medical costs, and the funds roll over year after year, providing a buffer against rising healthcare expenses in retirement.

Medicare and Supplemental Insurance Options

Once you reach the age of 65, Medicare becomes your primary form of health insurance, but it's essential to understand that Medicare alone might not cover all of your medical expenses. There are several parts of Medicare, and each part covers different healthcare needs.

- **Medicare Part A** typically covers hospital stays, skilled nursing facilities, and hospice care.
- **Medicare Part B** is for outpatient care, doctor visits, and preventive services.
- **Medicare Part C** covers prescription drugs (Medicare Interactive, 2019).

Many people choose Medicare Advantage (Part C), which combines Parts A and B and often includes prescription drug coverage, along with extra benefits like dental and vision care. However, Medicare doesn't cover everything, such as long-term care, so it's essential to have a plan in place to address these coverage gaps. (Medicare Interactive, 2019).

This is where **supplemental insurance** comes into play. Medigap plans, which are sold by private insurance companies, are designed to cover the out-of-pocket expenses that traditional Medicare does not, such as deductibles and co-pays. There are different levels of Medigap coverage, so it's essential to choose a plan that fits your financial and healthcare needs (Medicare Interactive, 2019).

Additionally, long-term care insurance can be a valuable investment for covering expenses like in-home care, assisted living, or nursing homes, which Medicare doesn't pay for. Long-term care can be costly, so having insurance to cover these services ensures that your assets are protected if you ever require extended care.

Updating Estate Plans

Estate planning is a crucial component of financial management, especially as you age. It involves organizing your assets and ensuring that they are distributed according to your wishes after your death. Updates to your estate plan regularly ensure that it reflects your current wishes, protects your loved ones, and minimizes potential disputes.

Importance of Reviewing and Updating Wills, Trusts, and Beneficiary Designations

Your will and any trusts you establish form the backbone of your estate plan. A will outline how your assets will be distributed, and it allows you to appoint guardians for any dependents. Trusts, on the other hand, offer more flexibility and control over how and when your assets are distributed.

It's crucial to review and update your will and trusts periodically to reflect life changes, such as a marriage, divorce, birth of a child, or a significant shift in your financial situation. If these documents are not up-to-date, your assets may not be distributed as you intended, which could create unnecessary complications for your heirs.

Beneficiary designations, such as those on retirement accounts or life insurance policies, also need to be reviewed regularly. These designations override what is stated in your will, so it's critical to make sure they are consistent with your current wishes. Outdated beneficiary designations, such as a former spouse being listed on a life insurance policy, can lead to unintended consequences.

Keeping these documents current ensures that your estate will be handled according to your intentions and provides clarity for your loved ones, avoiding potential legal disputes or confusion.

Planning for Potential Long-Term Care and Preserving Your Legacy

Long-term care is one of the most significant financial risks that retirees face. Without a plan, the costs associated with in-home care, assisted living, or nursing homes can quickly erode your savings. The first step in preparing for this is to assess whether you may need long-term care in the future. Conditions such as Alzheimer's, Parkinson's disease, or severe physical disabilities often require long-term care (Needham, 2024).

One option is to purchase long-term care insurance, which helps cover the cost of these services. While the premiums can be expensive, it's worth considering if your family has a history of medical conditions that could require extended care.

In addition to addressing long-term care needs, estate planning involves preserving your legacy. This includes passing on assets to your heirs, charitable giving, or ensuring that your personal values are reflected in how your estate is distributed. Trusts can play a vital role in legacy planning. A **revocable trust** allows you to retain control over your assets while you are alive and helps avoid probate, ensuring a smoother transition of your wealth to your heirs. An **irrevocable trust**, on the other hand, can offer tax benefits and protect your assets from creditors (Needham, 2024).

Estate planning also includes considering tax implications. Proper planning can help minimize estate taxes and ensure that more of your assets go to your beneficiaries rather than to the government. This is especially important if you have a substantial estate that may be subject to federal or state estate taxes (Needham, 2024).

Incorporating charitable giving into your estate plan is another way to preserve your legacy. Many people choose to leave a portion of their estate to charitable organizations, either through direct bequests in their wills or by setting up charitable trusts. This allows you to support causes that are important to you and may also provide tax benefits for your estate (Needham, 2024).

Chapter 3:

Your Family Could Use a Little Help—But Just a Little!

Retirement is often viewed as a time to enjoy personal freedom, a period to finally focus on your own happiness and do the things you've always wanted to do. However, for many people, retirement can also bring new responsibilities within the family. You might find yourself helping out your adult children, looking after grandchildren, or supporting aging relatives. While these roles can be rewarding and bring a sense of fulfillment, they can also become demanding if not managed properly.

It's really important to find a balance. Of course, you want to be there for your family, but you also need to make sure you are protecting your own time and making the most of your retirement. Balancing the needs of your loved ones with your own personal time is something many retirees struggle with. You want to help, but you don't want to lose sight of the things that bring you joy and fulfillment.

One of the gifts of retirement is the time to be more present for special moments with your family—like attending your grandchildren's sports activities or school events, even the ones that would have fallen during your working hours. It's a unique joy to be able to show up for these moments without the worry of missing out because you're still at work.

The first step in finding this balance is setting clear boundaries. This way, you can be supportive without giving up too much of your own time and energy. It's also helpful to prioritize family requests and delegate tasks when needed. Not everything has to fall on you. Sharing responsibilities with other family members or using resources like daycare for grandchildren can make a big difference.

Equally important is scheduling time for yourself. Whether it's doing a hobby you love, spending time with friends, or just taking a quiet moment for yourself, it's crucial to make sure you are still able to enjoy the things that make you happy.

The Importance of Boundaries in Retirement

As you approach retirement, you might picture this phase of life as a time to relax, explore new hobbies, and enjoy the freedom that comes after years of work. However, one key aspect that often goes unnoticed is the importance of setting boundaries. Without boundaries, it's easy for your time and energy to be consumed by the needs of others, leaving you feeling overwhelmed and perhaps a bit lost. Establishing clear, healthy boundaries allows you to protect your well-being, maintain balance, and truly enjoy the life you've worked so hard to reach.

Redefining Roles and Responsibilities After Retirement

Transitioning from a full-time career to retirement is, without a doubt, a major life change. After years of structure and routine, where you've had clear responsibilities tied to your job, retirement can feel like entering a completely new world. Suddenly, you find yourself with more time on your hands, and that shift can create the impression for others—especially family members—that you are always available. It's not uncommon for a family to assume that since you're no longer working, you can easily take on extra responsibilities, such as babysitting grandchildren, helping with errands, or even taking on caregiving roles for older relatives.

While it's natural to want to be there for your loved ones, retirement isn't meant to be an open invitation for everyone to rely on you all the time. It's important to take a step back and redefine what your role in the family looks like now that you are retired. After all, retirement is about you, too. It's a time to focus on what makes you happy and fulfilled, not just about taking care of others.

For example, imagine if your children assume you'll be available at the drop of a hat to watch the grandkids while they handle other tasks. It's easy to see how this could quickly become overwhelming, especially if it happens more frequently than expected. To avoid this, it's really helpful to have an open conversation with your family explaining what you are willing and able to do during this phase of your life. It's not that you don't want to help—it's about ensuring that you have the time to enjoy your own retirement as well. This way, everyone knows what to expect, and there's no frustration or disappointment on either side.

Avoiding Burnout

One of the most critical reasons for setting boundaries in retirement is to prevent burnout. While retirement should be a time of peace and enjoyment, it can quickly become a source of stress if you're constantly trying to meet the needs of everyone around you. Taking on too many responsibilities can leave you feeling exhausted, both mentally and physically.

Retirement burnout is something that can sneak up on you. You may start by saying yes to a few small requests, but over time, these can add up, and before you know it, your days are packed with obligations. This can lead to frustration, irritability, and even feelings of resentment. It's easy to feel like you're being pulled in all directions, and that's the last thing anyone wants during what's supposed to be a fulfilling stage of life.

To avoid burnout, it's essential to be mindful of your limits. Take time to reflect on how much responsibility you're comfortable with, and don't be afraid to say no when something feels like it's too much. For instance, if you enjoy helping out with the grandchildren but find that it's taking up most of your free time, consider setting a specific schedule that works for both you and your family. Maybe you agree to watch them one or two days a week, but beyond that, you reserve time for yourself. It's all about finding a balance that allows you to help without feeling overextended.

Establishing boundaries doesn't mean you're being selfish or that you don't care about your family. In fact, by protecting your time and energy, you're ensuring that when you do help, you're doing so from a place of love and care, not out of obligation or exhaustion. Your retirement is a precious time that you've earned, and it's important to guard that time so you can pursue the activities and experiences that bring you joy.

You're Not a Full-Time Caregiver

One of the most important shifts you need to make is understanding that you are not the family's full-time caregiver. It can be difficult to let go of that sense of responsibility, especially if you've always been the person others turn to in times of need. But retirement is a new chapter, and it's essential to recognize that while you can still be supportive, you don't need to take on the role of solving every problem or being the default caretaker for everyone in your life.

For many retirees, particularly those who have spent years taking care of their children or even elderly parents, this shift can feel uncomfortable at first. You might worry that by stepping back, you're letting people down. However, it's important to remember that setting boundaries is not about abandoning your family. It's about communicating clearly and ensuring that you have the space to enjoy your own life without being overwhelmed by the demands of others.

Take, for example, the common scenario of being asked to care for grandchildren regularly. While you may enjoy spending time with them, it's important to communicate that you are not available every day and that your retirement should include time for you to rest, travel, or pursue hobbies that you've been waiting for years to enjoy. Setting these boundaries early on will help avoid misunderstandings and resentment later.

It's also important to empower other family members to share responsibilities. For instance, if you've been the primary caregiver for an aging parent, now might be the time to have a family discussion about how others can step in to help. This not only relieves some of the pressure on you but also allows other family members to play a more active role in caregiving. It's about creating a balanced, healthy dynamic where everyone contributes rather than relying on you to carry the load.

Understanding Your Own Needs and Desires

As you move into retirement, it becomes increasingly important to take the time to really understand your own needs and desires. After spending years balancing work, family, and other commitments, this phase offers a unique opportunity to pause and reflect on what truly brings you joy and fulfillment. You may find that some of your past interests continue to excite you, or you may feel drawn to explore new activities. Either way, before you start establishing boundaries, it's essential to take stock of what makes you feel content, energized, and at peace.

Recognizing the activities that bring you happiness is the first step in crafting a retirement that suits your vision. As you become more in tune with what fulfills you, it becomes much easier to set limits on what you're willing to take on for others, ensuring that your retirement is centered around your personal happiness and well-being.

The Importance of Personal Time

Once you've clarified your needs and desires, the next step is protecting your personal time. After years of balancing professional and family responsibilities, retirement is the perfect moment to prioritize time for yourself. While it might seem like you have more time than ever before, that can quickly slip away if you don't set boundaries to protect it.

Personal time is a necessity for maintaining mental clarity, happiness, and overall satisfaction with life. Having this time allows you to recharge and reconnect with yourself, especially after years of focusing on others. Think about it: when you carve out moments just for yourself, you give your mind and body the space to rest. These moments of rest and reflection help reduce stress and improve your overall mood, leaving you feeling more refreshed and ready to take on the rest of your day.

It's easy to underestimate how important personal time can be. But when you don't allow yourself this space, it can quickly lead to burnout or feelings of being overwhelmed, even in retirement. Protecting your personal time should be one of your top priorities. This might mean setting aside a few hours each day for activities you enjoy, or it could mean scheduling larger blocks of time throughout the week. What's important is that this time is non-negotiable—it's time for you and no one else.

When you protect your personal time, you're also protecting your overall well-being. It helps you maintain a sense of balance in your life, ensuring that your retirement is as fulfilling and relaxing as you imagined it would be.

Balancing the Urge to Help With Personal Fulfillment

For many people, especially those who have spent years caring for family or working in roles where they provided for others, the urge to continue helping can be strong, even after retirement. It's natural to want to be there for your loved ones and to offer support when they need it, but retirement is also the time to focus on yourself. Striking a balance between helping others and ensuring your own personal fulfillment is key to enjoying a well-rounded and satisfying retirement.

One of the challenges many retirees face is the temptation to say "yes" to every request that comes their way. You might find yourself frequently called upon to babysit grandchildren, help out with household tasks, or provide advice on family matters. While it can feel rewarding to lend a hand, it's essential to recognize when these commitments start to interfere with your own goals and desires. Over time, saying "yes" too often can leave you feeling drained and can prevent you from focusing on the things that bring you personal joy.

To find the right balance, it's important to be honest with yourself about how much time and energy you have to give. It's perfectly okay to want to help your family, but it's also okay to set limits. For example, you might decide to help with childcare one day a week but make it clear that the rest of your time is reserved for your own projects or relaxation. This allows you to offer support without sacrificing your own needs.

Another way to maintain balance is by involving your family in conversations about your new role in retirement. Let them know what your priorities are and explain how you'd like to spend your time. This not only helps set clear expectations but also ensures that your family understands that while you're happy to help, your retirement is a time for you to pursue personal fulfillment as well.

Ultimately, it's about giving yourself permission to prioritize your own happiness. There's no need to feel guilty about focusing on yourself—you've earned this time. Retirement is the perfect opportunity to embrace your own interests and goals, and finding the right balance between helping others and dedicating time to your own personal fulfillment is crucial for long-term happiness.

Identifying Family Expectations and Potential Conflicts

Once you retire, it's common for family members to assume that you now have all the time in the world. This assumption often brings with it a range of unspoken expectations. Without even realizing it, family members may start to rely on you for various tasks, such as babysitting grandchildren, running errands, or helping out with small but frequent chores. They might feel that since you're no longer tied to a full-time job, you must have the freedom to assist whenever they need, without considering that you might have other plans for your time.

These expectations can be tricky to navigate, especially when they're not clearly communicated. Family members may genuinely believe that you're happy to help, or they might think their requests are small and easy to fulfill. Yet, over time, these small tasks can accumulate, leaving you with little time for yourself. Many retirees find themselves busier than ever, but not necessarily with the activities they envisioned doing when they first left the workforce.

It's not that these requests are made with ill intentions—on the contrary, they often stem from the closeness of family relationships. However, without addressing these unspoken expectations, they can lead to a situation where you feel overwhelmed or even resentful as you try to balance your desire to help with your need for personal time.

Communicating Boundaries Early On

The key to avoiding misunderstandings and conflicts later on is to establish boundaries from the very beginning. It can be easy to fall into the trap of saying yes to every request, especially if you're trying to be helpful or don't want to disappoint your family. However, it's important to remember that your time is now your own, and it's perfectly reasonable to set limits on how much of it you dedicate to others.

One of the best ways to do this is by having an open conversation with your family early on. Let them know how excited you are to spend time with them, but also explain that you have personal interests and goals that you want to pursue in retirement. For example, you might be looking forward to traveling, engaging in a new hobby, or simply enjoying some well-earned relaxation. By discussing your boundaries in a calm and positive way, you can prevent future conflicts and ensure that everyone is on the same page.

During these conversations, it's helpful to be clear about what you can and cannot do. Perhaps you're happy to babysit your grandchildren once or twice a week, but you don't want to take on the role of a full-time caregiver. Or maybe you're willing to help out with errands occasionally, but you don't want it to become a daily responsibility. By setting these expectations early, you give your family a better understanding of your availability, and they are less likely to ask for more than you are comfortable giving.

Dealing With Family Pushback

Even with the best intentions, setting boundaries can sometimes lead to pushback from family members. They might feel disappointed or confused when you tell them that you're not able to help as much as they expected. In some cases, they may even express feelings of hurt, especially if they were counting on your support.

When this happens, it's important to approach the situation with empathy. Acknowledge their feelings and let them know that you understand where they're coming from. At the same time, calmly explain why it's important for you to have personal time and to pursue your own interests. It can help to remind them that just because you're retired doesn't mean you're always available and that you still need time for yourself to recharge and enjoy life.

Finding a balance is crucial here. If a family member is particularly upset about your boundaries, consider offering a compromise that works for both of you. For example, if they were hoping for your help on a daily basis, you might suggest specific days or times when you can assist rather than committing to an open-ended schedule. This way, you can offer support while still protecting your own time and energy.

It's worth noting that resistance to boundaries is often temporary. Once your family members understand that you're setting these limits not out of a lack of care but to ensure your own well-being, they are more likely to respect your decisions. Over time, they will likely adjust their expectations and find other solutions for the tasks they were initially hoping you would take on.

The Components of a Healthy Boundary

Healthy boundaries are built on several key components, each of which plays an important role in ensuring they are effective and respected. First, **verbal communication** is essential. This means clearly stating what you can and cannot do, leaving no room for misinterpretation. For instance, if a family member frequently asks you to babysit, you could say, "I love spending time with the kids, but I need to reserve some days for my own activities." Being direct like this without being confrontational helps prevent future misunderstandings.

Non-verbal cues also support your boundaries. Often, how you deliver your message is just as important as the words you choose. If your body language or tone of voice seems uncertain, it may give the impression that your boundary is flexible. For example, if you say you're unavailable for an outing, but your tone is hesitant or apologetic, it could leave the other person thinking that you might change your mind. Standing firm, using steady eye contact, and speaking with a calm, assured tone can reinforce the boundary you are setting.

Finally, **consistency** is the key to maintaining healthy boundaries. It's natural to want to be flexible for the sake of keeping peace, but if you bend your rules too often, family members might not take your boundaries seriously. For instance, if you've decided to keep Sundays free for yourself but find yourself agreeing to family requests more often than not, your boundary will start to lose its meaning. Consistently following through on your limits helps others respect them, and over time, they will understand that your boundaries are not up for negotiation.

Defining Specific Boundaries for Common Family Requests

One of the biggest challenges retirees face is handling the various requests from family members. These can range from practical help like babysitting and errands to more sensitive issues such as financial support. While these requests are often well-intentioned, they can quickly become overwhelming without clear boundaries.

Take, for instance, a frequent issue of being asked for financial assistance. After retirement, your income may be more limited, and you might need to prioritize your own financial security. A boundary for this situation might sound like, "I can help with smaller expenses, but I'm not able to provide regular financial support." It's also important to remember that setting boundaries is about ensuring that the support you offer is sustainable for you. You may still want to help with family needs, but defining the *when* and *how* ensures that you don't feel overburdened or taken for granted.

Boundaries That Empower vs. Boundaries That Restrict

A common misconception about boundaries is that they create distance or hinder close relationships, but in reality, healthy boundaries actually strengthen those connections. When set thoughtfully, boundaries empower both you and your family members, allowing relationships to flourish in a balanced way.

For you, boundaries create space for self-care and personal fulfillment. After years of working and perhaps prioritizing others' needs, retirement offers a chance to rediscover what truly brings you joy. Setting boundaries ensures that you have the energy to pursue these things without feeling constantly pulled in different directions by family demands.

At the same time, boundaries empower your family members by encouraging them to respect your time and independence. When you set clear expectations, they are more likely to plan ahead and be mindful of your availability. For example, if you've made it clear that weekends are for your personal projects, your children or grandchildren might start making alternative arrangements for their weekend plans, understanding that your time is important too. This fosters a sense of mutual respect and responsibility, allowing the relationship to grow in a healthy way.

Conversely, boundaries that are overly rigid or unclear can indeed create distance and tension. If you set a boundary but fail to communicate the reasons behind it, or if you enforce it harshly, it can leave family members feeling rejected or hurt. This is why it's important to approach boundary-setting with compassion. Explain your reasons gently, and be open to hearing their perspective as well. For instance, instead of saying, "I can't help you," you might say, "I'd love to help, but I also need time to take care of my own needs. Let's see if we can find a solution that works for both of us."

Techniques for Effective Communication

When it comes to setting and maintaining boundaries, communication plays an essential role in ensuring that those around you understand and respect your needs. How you communicate boundaries can either strengthen relationships or, if not handled carefully, lead to misunderstandings. Finding the right words, managing feelings of guilt, and learning how and when to compromise are crucial aspects of communicating in a way that is both kind and assertive.

Finding the Right Words to Express Boundaries

Expressing boundaries in a clear manner can often feel challenging, especially when you want to be firm about your limits but still maintain a sense of care for the other person's feelings. It can feel like a delicate balance act, but using the right language can make all the difference. By focusing on **"I" statements**, you can communicate your needs in a way that centers on your experience rather than pointing fingers. For example, instead of saying something like, "You always expect me to be available," you could say, "I feel overwhelmed when I don't have enough time to myself, and I need some downtime on the weekends." This phrasing shifts the focus onto your personal need for space, making it clear that the boundary is about your well-being, not about accusing the other person of doing something wrong.

Being **specific** is also crucial. Vague statements like, "I need some space," can leave others uncertain about how they should respond. Instead, saying, "I need my afternoons free, but I'm happy to help in the mornings," gives clear guidance and helps the other person understand your boundary more effectively. By being direct yet thoughtful, you ensure that your limits are understood without causing unnecessary tension.

In addition to the words you use, **body language** can speak volumes. Even if you choose your words carefully, your boundary may not come across effectively if your posture or tone conveys uncertainty. Standing tall, making eye contact, and using a calm but steady voice can reinforce your message, showing that you are serious about your boundaries. At the same time, softening your tone and offering a kind smile when appropriate can help maintain warmth in the conversation, ensuring the other person doesn't feel shut out or alienated.

Moreover, it's helpful to **acknowledge the other person's needs** while setting your own boundaries. You could say something like, "I know you're in a tough spot right now, and I wish I could do more, but I need to make sure I have enough time to rest. I can't take on this extra task at the moment." This type of phrasing shows empathy, which can make it easier for the other person to accept your boundaries.

Setting Boundaries Without Guilt

For many people, feelings of guilt become a major obstacle when setting boundaries. This often comes from a fear of letting others down or being perceived as selfish. It can be especially difficult if you've spent much of your life putting others' needs ahead of your own. However, it's important to remember that **setting boundaries is an act of self-care**, not selfishness. By establishing and maintaining healthy boundaries, you are protecting your own emotional and mental well-being, which ultimately allows you to be more present and engaged in your relationships.

Guilt often arises when we feel like we are disappointing others by not fulfilling their expectations. For instance, you might feel guilty for turning down a family member's request for help, especially if they seem upset or disappointed. However, it's helpful to **reframe the situation** and remind yourself that by setting boundaries, you are not saying no to the person; you are simply prioritizing your needs so that you don't overextend yourself. It's okay to recognize that you have limits, and maintaining those limits is necessary for your well-being.

Another way to reduce guilt is to understand that **everyone has boundaries**, even if they are not always clearly stated. Just as you respect other people's limits, you deserve the same in return. If the guilt feels overwhelming, it may help to remind yourself that setting boundaries is a way to **protect your energy and prevent burnout**. A simple reminder, such as, "I need to take care of myself first," can help shift your mindset when feelings of guilt start to surface.

In fact, when you set boundaries, you are laying the groundwork for healthier, more balanced relationships. By communicating your limits, you avoid the buildup of resentment that often comes from constantly saying yes to things that drain your energy. **Long-term boundaries create stronger relationships** because they allow you to be present without feeling overwhelmed or exploited.

It's also essential to **practice self-compassion** during this process. Setting boundaries may feel uncomfortable at first, especially if you're not used to saying no. Remind yourself that it's okay to feel uneasy when you're learning a new skill. Over time, the more you practice setting boundaries, the more natural it will feel and the less guilt you'll experience.

When and How to Compromise

While setting clear boundaries is important, there are times when **compromise** can lead to better outcomes for everyone involved. Compromise doesn't mean abandoning your needs; instead, it's about finding a middle ground that works for both you and the other person.

The first step in compromising is recognizing that **not every situation requires a strict boundary**. For example, if a friend asks for help moving on a day when you've planned some personal time, you might consider whether helping them would be manageable. If doing so wouldn't significantly disrupt your plans or well-being, it might be an opportunity to adjust your boundaries slightly.

When you decide to compromise, it's important to **negotiate openly**. Clearly state what you are willing to offer while still maintaining respect for your own limits. For instance, if a family member asks for a favor that you can't fully accommodate, you could say, "I can't help the whole day, but I can assist for a few hours in the morning." This way, you show your willingness to be flexible without overcommitting.

Effective compromises are those that feel mutually beneficial. This means that both parties feel heard and respected in the decision. You can achieve this by being open about your needs and encouraging the other person to share theirs. A collaborative approach can help both sides feel like they are working toward a common goal rather than one person giving up too much.

It's also crucial to **avoid compromising out of guilt**. If you feel pressured to give in simply because you don't want to disappoint someone, then the compromise may not be truly balanced. Before agreeing to any adjustment, ask yourself if the compromise feels right. If it does, proceed with confidence. But if you feel uneasy, it might be worth reevaluating whether this is the right situation to compromise.

Compromise, when done thoughtfully, can **strengthen relationships**. It shows that you are willing to be flexible and considerate of the other person's needs while still respecting your own boundaries. This can build trust and deepen mutual respect. However, the key to a successful compromise is ensuring that it doesn't leave you feeling overburdened or resentful. By maintaining a balance between assertiveness and flexibility, you can navigate family dynamics and social situations more smoothly, creating an environment where both parties feel valued.

Dealing With Boundary Violations

While boundaries are key to ensuring that your personal needs are met, there will inevitably be situations where those boundaries are crossed. Whether the violation is intentional or not, it can lead to frustration, conflict, and even resentment if not managed properly. Learning how to handle boundary violations in a calm and constructive way is crucial to protecting your emotional well-being and maintaining harmony within your family.

Recognizing When Boundaries Are Being Crossed

One of the first steps in dealing with boundary violations is to become aware of when your limits are being crossed. It might sound simple, but boundary violations are not always easy to spot, especially when they happen gradually or are disguised as well-meaning requests. For example, a family member might ask you to help with small tasks—like watching their children for an hour or running a quick errand—and at first, this might seem harmless. However, when those "small" requests start to pile up, and you find yourself feeling overwhelmed, it's a clear sign that your boundaries are not being respected.

Sometimes, boundary violations are subtle and can easily go unnoticed until you begin to feel the emotional effects. You might start to notice feelings of irritation, fatigue, or even resentment after spending time with certain family members. These emotions are often red flags that something is off and that your boundaries may have been crossed. For instance, if a family member regularly asks for favors but never seems to respect your time or availability, you might begin to feel taken advantage of. Recognizing these feelings early on is key to addressing the issue before it escalates.

It's also important to remember that some family members may unintentionally cross boundaries simply because they are not aware of them. They might not realize that what they're asking of you is too much or that they are overstepping in some way. In these cases, it's essential to be mindful of your own emotional reactions and use them as signals to assess whether a boundary has been crossed.

Handling Conflicts and Resentments

When a boundary is crossed, it can quickly lead to conflicts or feelings of resentment, especially if the issue is not addressed early on. For many people, dealing with these conflicts can be challenging because it often involves uncomfortable conversations with loved ones. However, addressing boundary violations calmly and constructively is the best way to prevent further emotional strain and protect your relationships.

One of the most effective ways to handle boundary violations is through clear and direct communication. This doesn't mean being confrontational or blaming the other person, but rather expressing how their actions have affected you in a way that invites understanding and cooperation. For example, instead of saying something like, "You never respect my time," which can feel accusatory, you could say, "I've noticed that when I'm asked to help with errands every week, it's starting to feel overwhelming. I need some time for myself." By focusing on your own feelings and experiences, you create a more constructive dialogue that encourages problem-solving rather than defensiveness.

In some cases, family members might not realize they've crossed a boundary, so giving them the opportunity to understand your perspective can lead to a positive outcome. They may not have intended to overstep and might be open to adjusting their behavior once they understand how it's affecting them. That said, it's equally important to listen to their perspective as well. Open dialogue can help both parties better understand each other's needs and find a solution that works for everyone.

However, it's also possible that not every conversation will go smoothly. Some family members may push back against your boundaries, especially if they're used to a certain level of access to your time or energy. When this happens, it's important to remain calm and firm in your stance. It can be tempting to give in or feel guilty for standing your ground, but it's essential to remember why you set those boundaries in the first place. Staying consistent in how you communicate and uphold your boundaries helps reinforce their importance and ensures that you're not compromising your own well-being.

Enforcing Consequences

Setting boundaries is a crucial first step but only part of the equation. The real challenge often comes when those boundaries are repeatedly ignored or violated. In these situations, enforcing consequences is necessary to ensure your limits are respected. While enforcing consequences might sound harsh, it's actually an important way to protect your own emotional health and communicate to others that your boundaries are non-negotiable.

Consequences don't have to be punitive or harsh, but they should be clear and consistent. For example, if you've asked a family member not to drop by your house unannounced and they continue to do so, a consequence could be simply not answering the door when they arrive unexpectedly. Or, if a relative constantly asks for financial assistance despite your having set a boundary around money, you might decide to stop engaging in conversations about money altogether. These types of consequences reinforce that your boundaries are serious and not to be overlooked.

It's also important to communicate these consequences ahead of time so the other person is aware of the potential outcomes. For instance, you might say, "If you continue to call me after 8 p.m. when I've asked for quiet time, I won't be able to answer the phone." This not only sets a clear expectation but also gives the other person a chance to adjust their behavior before any action is taken.

Enforcing consequences can be uncomfortable, especially when dealing with close family members, but it's a necessary step in maintaining healthy relationships. If your boundaries are repeatedly violated without any consequences, it sends the message that your limits aren't important, which can lead to ongoing issues and emotional exhaustion.

In some cases, repeated boundary violations may lead you to limit or even cut off contact with certain family members. This is often a last resort, but in situations where your emotional health is at risk, it may be the best course of action. If, for example, a family member consistently disrespects your personal space or crosses emotional boundaries despite numerous conversations and consequences, you might decide that limiting your interactions with them is the only way to protect yourself. While this can be a difficult decision, it's important to prioritize your mental and emotional health above all else.

Balancing Support and Independence

It's natural to want to assist your loved ones, but it's equally important to maintain your own sense of autonomy. This means figuring out how to offer help without becoming the go-to solution for every challenge, fostering self-sufficiency in those around you, and, perhaps most difficult of all, learning to let go when necessary. Just because you've set boundaries doesn't mean you can't support your family when they need it. However, it's essential to strike a balance between being there for your loved ones and allowing them to solve problems on their own. You don't want to become the first person they turn to for every little issue, as that can quickly become overwhelming, and over time, it might encourage dependency rather than independence.

One of the best ways to help without taking over is to offer advice rather than action. For example, if your adult child is facing a financial decision, you might offer to sit with them and go through their budget or explore different financial options together instead of directly stepping in with financial assistance. This way, you are guiding them through the process but still letting them take responsibility for their decisions.

Another practical strategy is to be mindful of how often you offer help. It's perfectly fine to lend a hand now and then, but if you find yourself consistently saying "yes" to every request, it might be time to step back a bit. Maybe you agree to help with babysitting once a week, but not every time they ask. Setting a limit ensures that you're not constantly on call and still have time for yourself. This balance allows you to be supportive while keeping your independence intact.

Clear communication is key here. Let your family know that while you're more than happy to help when you can, you also need to make time for your own needs and activities. When your boundaries are communicated clearly, your loved ones are more likely to respect them and plan accordingly.

Fostering Self-Sufficiency in Family Members

Helping your family members become more self-reliant is not only beneficial for them, but it's also crucial for maintaining your own independence. When you step back a little, you give them the opportunity to learn how to handle their own challenges, which fosters growth and resilience. The goal here is to empower them to solve problems on their own, with your support as a backup rather than the primary solution.

One way to foster self-sufficiency is to ask guiding questions when they come to you for advice. For instance, instead of immediately giving a solution, you might ask, "What do you think you should do next?" or "How have you handled a situation like this before?" By prompting them to think through the problem themselves, you're encouraging them to take ownership of the solution. You can always offer advice or confirm their choices, but the focus should be on helping them develop the skills to manage these situations independently.

Providing resources is another excellent way to help without over-involvement. If they're struggling with managing time or juggling responsibilities, suggesting organizational tools like planners or apps can be a great way to offer assistance.

Similarly, leading by example is one of the most effective ways to encourage self-reliance. When your family sees you maintaining your own responsibilities, making decisions that honor your boundaries, and handling challenges in a balanced way, they are more likely to follow suit. Your actions demonstrate that it's possible to be independent while still being there for others in a meaningful way.

Learning to Let Go

Perhaps the hardest part of balancing support and independence is learning to step back when your loved ones are struggling. It's natural to want to protect those we care about from difficulties, but sometimes the best way to help is to allow them to face challenges on their own.

This isn't about abandoning them; rather, it's about trusting that they have the ability to handle things and grow from the experience.

There will be moments when your family members need to navigate situations without your direct involvement, whether it's a financial setback, a difficult relationship issue, or learning to manage their own household. While it might be tough to watch them face these difficulties, it's important to remember that struggle can lead to growth and resilience. Your loved ones may learn more from handling these challenges on their own than they ever would if you stepped in to fix things every time.

Stepping back doesn't mean you can't still offer emotional support. You can check in, ask how things are going, and offer encouragement when needed. But it's important to resist the urge to take over. It's about being there to listen rather than to solve every problem.

Letting go also means learning to manage any guilt you might feel about not stepping in. It's easy to think that by not helping, you're somehow failing them, but in reality, you're giving them the chance to grow. Remind yourself that allowing them to work through difficulties independently is an essential part of their development. As hard as it may be, you're helping them build the confidence they need to handle challenges in the future.

Creating a New Family Dynamic Post-Retirement

Retirement is a significant transition, and it often brings changes not only in your daily routine but also in your relationships, especially with your family. As you move away from the structured demands of work, you may find yourself adjusting to a new rhythm of life. At the same time, your adult children are likely in the midst of their own busy lives, building careers and families, or pursuing other personal goals. This phase of life presents a unique opportunity to redefine family dynamics, but it also requires setting boundaries to maintain balance and harmony.

Redefining Relationships With Adult Children

One of the first things to consider after retirement is how your relationship with your adult children may evolve. In many ways, this period can feel like a new chapter for both you and them. As they continue to grow in their independence, whether that means navigating their careers or raising families of their own, they might still turn to you for guidance or support. And while it is natural to want to help, especially as a parent, retirement is also a time for you to prioritize your own needs and interests.

It's not uncommon for adult children to expect their retired parents to be available more often. But just because you may have more free time doesn't mean you are obligated to fill every request. The goal here is to create a balance where you can still offer support without sacrificing your newfound freedom. It's okay to say no sometimes, and it's equally okay to communicate that your time is valuable, too. When approached with kindness and clarity, these boundaries will actually strengthen your relationship with your adult children as they learn to respect your time and decisions while still feeling supported.

Building Healthy, Interdependent Relationships

Interdependence is about supporting each other in meaningful ways but without becoming overly reliant on one another. It allows for mutual care and assistance while still respecting each person's need for independence. For many retirees, there's a fine line between being supportive and becoming the "go-to" solution for every problem their children face. While you might be eager to help, it's important to remember that part of supporting your adult children is allowing them to solve their own problems. Encouraging self-sufficiency can be one of the most loving things you can do. You are helping them to grow and build resilience by not always stepping in to "fix" things.

This doesn't mean withdrawing support altogether, but rather shifting the nature of your help. For instance, if your child comes to you for advice on a personal or financial matter, you can offer guidance but avoid taking over. Ask open-ended questions that encourage them to think through their decisions, such as "What options have you considered?" or "How do you feel about that approach?" By fostering this kind of dialogue, you help them become more confident in their decision-making process while still being a source of wisdom and reassurance.

In building interdependent relationships, it's also crucial to maintain your own independence. Pursue your passions, hobbies, and social activities without feeling guilty. This doesn't just enrich your own life; it also models healthy behavior for your children, showing them the importance of having their own space and interests.

Reinforcing Boundaries With Time

One challenge that can arise post-retirement is the slow erosion of boundaries over time. Even if you set clear limits at the beginning, life changes—whether that's a new grandchild, a family crisis, or simply the passage of time—can cause those boundaries to blur. If you're not careful, you might find yourself gradually doing more than you originally intended, which can lead to feelings of frustration or even burnout.

That's why it's important to reinforce your boundaries consistently. If you've agreed to help out with family obligations, be clear about what that looks like in practice. It's perfectly acceptable to revisit and adjust boundaries as needed. You might say something like, "I love helping out with the kids, but I've noticed I'm feeling a bit stretched. Can we talk about finding a better balance?"

Boundaries are not set in stone—they need to evolve as life circumstances change. This is why ongoing communication is so essential. If something doesn't feel sustainable anymore, have a conversation with your family about how things can be adjusted. It's also important to be mindful of boundaries when it comes to financial support. Many retirees find themselves helping their adult children or grandchildren financially, but it's critical to ensure that this assistance doesn't jeopardize your own retirement security. Setting financial boundaries may feel uncomfortable at first, but it's crucial for maintaining your own well-being. Be honest about what you can afford to offer, and don't hesitate to say no if you feel the situation requires it.

Chapter 4:

Burnout is Real—Now It's Your Time to Rejuvenate

Burnout is something many of us experience at some point in life, but for those transitioning into retirement, it can feel more intense and overwhelming than expected. After years of dedicating so much time and energy to work, the idea of burnout can manifest not just physically but emotionally and mentally as well. Retirement, while often seen as a time of freedom and relaxation, can actually magnify these feelings, especially when the change from a structured, busy life to a quieter, more flexible one happens suddenly. This shift can leave many retirees feeling both exhausted and unsure of how to move forward.

However, it is essential to recognize that burnout is not a personal failure or weakness. In reality, it's the body and mind's natural way of signaling that they need a break—a chance to heal and restore. This signal is one that should be acknowledged, not ignored. Instead of pushing through the fatigue, the key to recovery lies in embracing rest and rejuvenation. Taking care of yourself during retirement isn't just about slowing down; it's about prioritizing activities and practices that support your overall well-being.

As you enter this new chapter of life, it's important to focus on the core pillars of recovery—rest, self-care, stress management, and maintaining social connections. Each of these elements plays a critical role in helping retirees not only recover from burnout but also create a fulfilling, vibrant life moving forward. After all, retirement should be a time to rediscover what brings joy and peace, allowing space for relaxation and reflection.

By tuning into these aspects of self-care, you can look forward to a healthier and happier future. Embracing the need for recovery isn't about giving up productivity; rather, it's about shifting perspectives. In this stage of life, taking the time to rest and focus on personal well-being is essential to living a life that is both meaningful and enjoyable. Rejuvenating now sets the foundation for experiencing retirement with a renewed sense of energy and purpose, making the years ahead as fulfilling as they deserve.

Prioritize Rest and Recovery

Understanding the importance of rest in recovery is crucial, especially for those who have spent decades in demanding work environments. Burnout, which accumulates over time, doesn't just affect a person physically. It seeps into the mind and emotions, creating a decp sense of exhaustion that touches every part of life. It's the kind of fatigue that isn't fixed by a single good night's sleep, and often, it's the result of pushing too hard for too long without adequate breaks. For many retirees, the shift from a busy work life to a quieter retirement can make these feelings even more pronounced.

After years of waking up to a strict schedule, meeting deadlines, and navigating the pressures of work, suddenly stepping into retirement can feel like hitting a wall. The body and mind, long accustomed to the hustle, might feel lost without that familiar structure, which often leads to a heightened awareness of the burnout that has been building up all along. Retirees might feel mentally drained, emotionally tired, and physically worn out even though they're no longer working. This transition can be overwhelming because, for many, it's the first time in decades that they've had the chance to really pause.

But burnout is more than just being tired—it's a state where the mind and body simply can't keep up with the demands placed on them. Over the years, this constant state of stress starts to chip away at energy levels, cognitive function, and even emotional resilience. That's why rest and recovery are so vital. When we talk about rest, we're not just referring to sleep, although sleep is a big part of it. We're talking about a broader sense of taking time to heal, both mentally and physically.

Rest allows the body and mind to repair themselves. For the body, rest helps restore energy reserves that are depleted during long periods of activity and stress. Muscles need time to heal, and the immune system requires downtime to rebuild and strengthen itself. Without adequate rest, these systems become worn out, leaving a person more vulnerable to illness and injury. Mentally, rest is equally important. The brain needs a break from the constant processing of information, and when it doesn't get this break, it can lead to issues with concentration, memory, and decision-making.

Sleep plays a huge role in recovery, especially for those in retirement. As we age, sleep becomes even more essential to our health and well-being. It's during sleep that the body undergoes many of its most important restorative processes. Sleep helps to solidify memories, supports cognitive function, and allows the body to recover from the physical wear and tear of the day. For retirees, maintaining good sleep hygiene becomes particularly important. Sleep hygiene refers to the habits and practices that ensure high-quality sleep. This can involve everything from keeping a regular sleep schedule to creating a relaxing bedtime routine.

One of the key challenges retirees face is ensuring they get enough high-quality sleep. It's not just about sleeping for a certain number of hours but also about making sure the sleep they're getting is restorative. For example, many older adults struggle with staying asleep through the night, which can lead to waking up feeling tired and unrested. To combat this, creating an environment that supports good sleep—such as keeping the bedroom dark, quiet, and cool—can make a significant difference.

Now, while sleep is undeniably important, it's only one piece of the puzzle. Recovery also involves something called intentional resting. This is where we actively create moments of rest throughout the day, beyond just sleeping at night. Intentional rest means taking deliberate steps to relax both physically and mentally, allowing the body and mind to disengage from stress. It's not something that happens by accident—you have to make time for it, plan for it, and understand what your body needs to fully rest.

Intentional resting can look different for everyone. For some, it might mean taking a walk in nature, breathing in the fresh air, and enjoying the quiet surroundings. For others, it could be sitting down with a book or practicing meditation to clear the mind. The point is to engage in activities that help you disconnect from stress and reconnect with a sense of calm. Unlike sleep, intentional resting is something you can control during the day, and it's just as vital for recovery as a good night's rest.

For retirees, this type of rest is especially important because it allows them to adjust to a slower pace of life without feeling guilty for not being as productive as they used to be. Many people, especially those who have spent decades in demanding careers, struggle with the idea of rest. They may feel like they always need to be doing something, and sitting still can make them uncomfortable. However, it's crucial to understand that resting is not the same as being lazy. In fact, resting is one of the most productive things you can do for your overall well-being.

One example of intentional rest is practicing mindfulness or meditation. These practices encourage the mind to focus on the present moment, letting go of the stresses and worries that can keep us constantly on edge. Just spending a few minutes each day sitting quietly and breathing deeply can have a profound impact on how you feel, both mentally and physically. Another way to incorporate intentional rest is through progressive muscle relaxation, where you slowly tense and then relax each muscle group in your body, allowing yourself to release built-up tension (National Institutes of Health, 2021).

For those who prefer a more active form of rest, gentle exercises like yoga or stretching can also provide both mental and physical benefits. Yoga, in particular, combines movement with mindfulness, helping to stretch and strengthen the body while calming the mind. These kinds of activities don't require much time or effort, but they can greatly impact how rested and rejuvenated you feel.

It's also important to understand that rest isn't something to feel guilty about. Many retirees may struggle with the transition from years of hard work to a more relaxed pace, feeling like they should still be doing more. But the truth is, after decades of productivity, your body and mind need—and deserve—a chance to rest. Allowing yourself to rest doesn't mean you're being unproductive; it means you're taking care of your health so that you can enjoy this new phase of life to the fullest.

Restorative Practices for the Retired Lifestyle

Restorative practices play a significant role in the retired lifestyle, providing a much-needed break from years of work-related stress and enabling both the body and mind to heal. After years of working, dealing with responsibilities, and constantly being on the go, retirees finally have the opportunity to slow down. However, adjusting to this slower pace and prioritizing rest is not always easy. It can take time to fully embrace the value of rest, but once these restorative practices are in place, they can transform the retirement experience into one filled with calm, clarity, and a renewed sense of energy.

One of the simplest yet most powerful ways to promote relaxation is through **deep breathing and relaxation techniques**. These exercises might seem basic at first, but they have a profound impact on calming both the mind and body. Breathing exercises work by slowing down the breath, which in turn signals to the nervous system that it's time to relax. For retirees, especially those who may still feel the remnants of workplace stress or who have difficulty letting go of anxious thoughts, deep breathing can be a helpful daily practice (Gotter, 2018).

One example of a deep breathing technique is called "4-7-8 breathing." In this exercise, you inhale deeply through your nose for a count of four, hold your breath for a count of seven, and then exhale slowly through your mouth for a count of eight. This controlled, rhythmic breathing helps to lower heart rate and reduce feelings of anxiety or restlessness. It's particularly useful during moments of stress or before bedtime when trying to wind down for the night. Breathing techniques like this one are simple, but they create a sense of peace and relaxation that can have lasting benefits (Gotter, 2018).

For retirees who sometimes feel sluggish during the day, **short naps** can be a wonderful way to restore energy without affecting the sleep cycle at night. Napping, when done correctly, can provide a powerful boost in alertness and mood. However, it's important to keep naps brief, usually between 15 to 30 minutes, to avoid entering deep sleep, which can leave you feeling groggy. Short naps fall into what's called the "light sleep" stage, which helps refresh the body and mind without interfering with nighttime sleep. These naps are ideal for those moments when you feel tired or drained but don't want to disrupt your usual sleep routine.

Research shows that napping not only recharges energy levels but also improves cognitive function, mood, and overall well-being. In fact, studies have linked regular, short naps to improved heart health and reduced stress levels (Lovato & Lack, 2010). For retirees, incorporating a brief nap into their daily routine can become a pleasant and revitalizing habit. Whether it's after lunch or during the early afternoon, a short nap can make a world of difference, leaving you feeling more refreshed and able to enjoy the rest of your day.

Beyond physical rest, **mindful rest practices** are another essential aspect of recovery. These practices are focused on achieving mental clarity and emotional balance through mindfulness exercises, such as guided imagery or body scanning. Mindful rest allows retirees to create moments of calm in their day, helping them disengage from stressors or anxious thoughts (Díaz-Silveira et al., 2020).

Guided imagery is a practice where you close your eyes and imagine yourself in a peaceful setting, such as walking through a quiet forest, sitting by a calm ocean, or resting in a cozy room. This mental imagery transports the mind away from everyday worries and helps reduce stress by focusing on calming positive thoughts. Over time, this practice can help retirees cultivate a sense of peace that carries over into other areas of life (Scott, 2005).

Another form of mindful rest is **body scanning**, which involves mentally scanning the body from head to toe, noticing any tension or discomfort. As you focus on each part of your body, you gradually release tension, helping your muscles and mind relax. Body scanning is especially beneficial for retirees because it encourages physical relaxation while also promoting mindfulness, making it easier to let go of stress and focus on the present moment. Both of these techniques are easy to practice and can be done in just a few minutes, but their impact can be felt long after the practice is over (Scott, 2024).

Equally important is the concept of **quiet time**, which often involves simply being still and creating space for peace. In our busy world, we often underestimate the value of moments spent doing nothing. However, quiet time is a crucial component of restful living, particularly for retirees. It can be as simple as sitting in a favorite chair with a cup of tea, spending time outdoors listening to the birds, or enjoying the stillness of a room without any distractions.

Quiet time allows the mind and body to relax without the pressure of tasks or responsibilities. It is a time to recharge mentally and emotionally. For retirees, these moments of solitude can bring a deeper sense of reflection, peace, and gratitude for the simplicity of life. Quiet time can also be spent in nature, where the sounds of the wind, trees, and wildlife create a natural environment for relaxation. The key is to embrace these moments of stillness and recognize their importance in restoring mental clarity and emotional well-being.

The Psychology of Letting Go

Transitioning into retirement also comes with its own set of psychological challenges, particularly when it comes to **letting go of a productivity-driven mindset**. After spending years in the workforce, where success is often measured by output and achievements, many retirees find it difficult to step away from this mentality. There's a kind of internal conflict that arises—a sense of guilt for resting or for not being as busy as before. Retirees often feel pressure, whether from society or themselves, to remain productive, even though they've earned the right to rest.

This guilt stems from the idea that rest equals laziness or that it's only something you do after you've completed all your "important" tasks. However, in retirement, it's vital to **reframe how we think about rest**. Rest is not a sign of laziness; it is a necessary part of maintaining long-term health and well-being. This is especially true after decades of hard work, where burnout and exhaustion have likely taken their toll on the body and mind. In fact, rest is a form of self-care, an investment in your future health, and an essential part of enjoying life to the fullest.

Overcoming this guilt requires a **shift in mindset**—understanding that rest is just as valuable as productivity. Retirees need to acknowledge that after decades of working, they deserve time to relax without feeling pressured to constantly achieve. Mental reframing is about recognizing that the value of rest lies in its ability to improve health, boost mood, and restore energy. It's important to remind yourself that rest is productive in its own way; it gives you the energy and clarity needed to fully enjoy the activities that bring you joy.

To help overcome the **societal pressure to stay busy**, retirees can focus on creating new routines that balance rest with fulfilling activities. For example, you might schedule a walk in the park in the morning, followed by some quiet time in the afternoon and a hobby or social activity later in the day. By establishing a routine that includes both rest and engagement, retirees can find a rhythm that feels satisfying without the need to constantly be doing something.

It's also helpful to look at rest as a way of preserving your well-being for the long term. Just as you wouldn't expect a car to run smoothly without regular maintenance, your body and mind need regular periods of rest to function at their best. This shift in perspective can help retirees embrace rest as a natural and essential part of life rather than something to feel guilty about.

Rediscovering Joy Through Self-Care

In retirement, there is a beautiful opportunity to slow down and reconnect with the things that once brought a sense of fulfillment or perhaps even explore new passions that you may not have had the time to pursue before. **Self-care for retirees** means finding joy in the small and simple pleasures that are often overlooked in the busy years of working and raising a family. It's about stepping back and giving yourself permission to enjoy life at a pace that feels right for you.

One of the key elements of self-care during retirement is taking the time to **reconnect with personal interests and passions**. After years of focusing on work, family, and the demands of everyday life, it can sometimes feel like we've lost touch with what really makes us happy. Self-care is all about rediscovering those hobbies or activities that bring joy, whether it's something as simple as tending to a garden, baking, or taking long, leisurely walks in the morning. These activities not only help retirees **reduce stress**, but they also boost mood and energy levels. In doing so, retirees find that their days feel more purposeful and that they are able to reconnect with a sense of calm and contentment.

Engaging in activities that you enjoy can also have a powerful effect on **overall happiness**. Whether it's painting, knitting, or spending time with grandchildren, these activities give retirees something to look forward to each day. They create a rhythm to life, one that is filled with moments of joy and satisfaction. Studies have shown that participating in enjoyable hobbies can lead to **improved mental health** by reducing feelings of anxiety or depression. When retirees focus on what brings them personal joy, they also find that they are better able to handle the emotional challenges that sometimes come with aging.

Beyond reducing stress and improving mood, self-care serves as a way to **cultivate gratitude and appreciation** for this new phase of life. Retirement is a time of transition, but it is also a time to reflect on the many things to be grateful for—the freedom to pursue passions without the constraints of a busy work schedule, the ability to spend time with loved ones, or simply the peace that comes from waking up without the pressure of deadlines. By embracing self-care, retirees allow themselves to slow down and savor these moments, fostering a deeper appreciation for life's blessings. In many ways, self-care becomes a practice of gratitude itself, reminding retirees to focus on the positive aspects of their lives.

Finding Your Flow

Retirement is a wonderful time to explore activities that not only provide relaxation but also offer a sense of fulfillment and purpose. Engaging in hobbies is not just a way to pass the time; it can actually help retirees **find their flow**, a state in which they are fully immersed in an activity, losing track of time as they become deeply absorbed in something that brings them satisfaction. Finding your flow means discovering activities that feel both enjoyable and meaningful.

Many retirees find that **physical activities** are an essential part of their self-care routine. Activities like **walking in nature**, **gentle yoga**, or even **swimming** are not only good for the body but also incredibly beneficial for the mind. For example, taking a walk through a local park or nature reserve allows retirees to connect with the natural world, helping them feel more grounded and at peace. The physical movement combined with the beauty of nature has a calming effect, easing stress and helping retirees feel more centered. Similarly, gentle yoga practices help retirees stay flexible and strong while also encouraging mindfulness and deep breathing. **Swimming**, especially in a pool or even in the ocean, offers a refreshing way to stay active without putting too much strain on the joints. The rhythm of swimming, combined with the buoyancy of the water, creates a soothing experience that leaves the body and mind feeling rejuvenated.

In addition to physical activities, many retirees find joy in **creative outlets**. Whether it's **painting**, **journaling**, **knitting**, or **playing music**, these activities allow retirees to express themselves in ways that are both fun and fulfilling. For example, painting or drawing provides an opportunity to focus on color, texture, and form, allowing retirees to immerse themselves in a world of creativity. The act of creating something with your own hands, whether it's a painting or a knitted scarf, brings a sense of accomplishment and pride. Similarly, **journaling** is a powerful way to reflect on thoughts and feelings, providing clarity and a space for self-expression. It allows retirees to explore their inner world, capture memories, or even write about new experiences and ideas. **Playing music** or learning a new instrument can also be deeply rewarding. Music has the power to lift the spirit and bring joy, whether it's through playing for yourself or sharing it with others.

Another important aspect of self-care during retirement is **reading and lifelong learning**. For many retirees, diving into a good book or exploring new knowledge can provide hours of relaxation and mental stimulation. Whether it's reading novels or non-fiction or learning about a subject you've always been curious about, books offer an escape and a way to keep the mind active. **Lifelong learning** also plays an essential role in maintaining mental agility. Retirees might choose to take up online courses, join book clubs, or attend lectures on topics they've always wanted to explore. These activities keep the brain engaged and provide a sense of accomplishment, helping retirees feel more fulfilled and mentally sharp.

One of the simplest yet most powerful ways to rejuvenate during retirement is through the **power of nature**. Spending time outdoors, whether it's sitting in a garden, taking a hike, or even just enjoying fresh air on the porch, has a profound effect on mental well-being. Nature has a way of calming the mind and reminding us of the beauty and simplicity of life. For retirees, being in nature offers a break from the hustle and bustle of daily life, providing an opportunity to slow down and appreciate the world around them. The sounds of birds, the feel of the breeze, and the sight of trees swaying in the wind all contribute to a deep sense of peace and relaxation. It's no wonder that many retirees find that spending time outdoors helps them feel more connected to themselves and the world.

Physical Self-care and Well-being

Taking care of the body becomes increasingly important as we age, and **physical self-care** is one of the key elements to maintaining overall health and well-being in retirement. This is not just about looking after physical health in the traditional sense but about nurturing the body in a way that promotes energy, flexibility, and comfort. **Good nutrition**, **adequate hydration**, and **gentle physical exercise** are essential parts of this approach, but there are also other forms of physical relaxation, such as **massages**, **baths**, and **stretching**, which all play a role in helping retirees maintain their mobility and prevent injury.

Importance of Nutrition, Hydration, and Gentle Physical Exercise

As we enter retirement, our nutritional needs shift slightly to support the aging body. While we no longer need to fuel long working hours, we do need to focus on maintaining energy levels and supporting our overall health. **Nutrition** plays a huge role in this. A balanced diet rich in fruits, vegetables, lean proteins, and whole grains can help boost energy, improve immune function, and keep the body functioning well. Many experts suggest that eating nutrient-dense foods, such as leafy greens, berries, and healthy fats like olive oil and nuts, can support brain function and overall vitality. Incorporating foods that are rich in fiber can help with digestion while also lowering the risk of certain chronic illnesses like heart disease or diabetes (Robinson, 2017).

Equally important is **hydration**. It's easy to overlook how much water we drink, but staying hydrated is vital to keeping the body running smoothly. Water helps regulate body temperature, keep joints lubricated, and even improve brain function. As we age, our sensation of thirst might decrease, meaning we may not feel the urge to drink as often as we should. However, drinking enough water—around **6 to 8 cups a day**—is crucial for avoiding dehydration, which can lead to headaches, fatigue, and a reduced ability to focus. Adding slices of lemon, cucumber, or even herbs like mint can make water more enjoyable to drink throughout the day. Simple habits, like carrying a reusable water bottle or setting reminders to drink regularly, can help maintain this essential part of physical self-care.

When it comes to **physical exercise**, many people might picture intense workouts, but for retirees, exercise doesn't have to be strenuous. In fact, **gentle physical activities** like walking, swimming, or light yoga can provide wonderful benefits. These activities help keep the muscles strong, improve circulation, and boost mood. Walking, for instance, is one of the easiest and most accessible exercises. A short daily walk outdoors can help strengthen the legs and back while also allowing you to enjoy the fresh air and nature. **Swimming** is another excellent option, as it is low-impact and gentle on the joints, making it ideal for those with arthritis or joint pain. The water provides natural resistance, helping to improve muscle tone and cardiovascular health without putting too much strain on the body.

Gentle yoga or stretching routines also play a critical role in maintaining flexibility and balance, which become more important with age. Yoga doesn't just stretch the muscles; it also strengthens them, improves balance, and encourages mindfulness through breathwork. This can help retirees not only feel more mobile but also more relaxed and centered throughout the day.

Taking Care of the Body Through Massages, Baths, Stretching, and Other Forms of Physical Relaxation

In addition to exercise and nutrition, **physical relaxation** is essential for overall well-being. Retirees may benefit greatly from incorporating **massages**, **baths**, and **stretching** into their routines. These activities provide deep relaxation while also helping to relieve muscle tension and improve circulation.

Massages, whether done by a professional or at home using simple tools, are a wonderful way to reduce tension in the muscles and increase blood flow. Regular massages can help alleviate pain caused by stiff muscles or joints, and they also promote relaxation by reducing levels of the stress hormone cortisol. This not only improves mood but can also lead to better sleep and reduced anxiety (Weerapong et al., 2005).

Similarly, taking time for a relaxing **bath** can have soothing effects on both the body and mind. A warm bath helps to relax muscles, ease tension, and improve circulation. Adding **Epsom salts** to the water can help to relieve aching muscles, while essential oils like lavender or chamomile can enhance the calming effect. Baths are a simple yet effective way to unwind at the end of the day, giving retirees the chance to relax both physically and mentally (Elliott, 2018).

Stretching is another important element of physical self-care that is often overlooked. Stretching helps to maintain flexibility, which naturally decreases as we age. A simple daily stretching routine can prevent stiffness and improve mobility, making everyday activities like bending down, reaching for something, or even walking more comfortable. Stretching also helps to increase blood flow to the muscles, which can aid in recovery after exercise and reduce the risk of injury (Lewine, 2022).

Incorporating **other forms of relaxation**, such as **deep breathing exercises** or **progressive muscle relaxation**, can also help retirees maintain a sense of calm and well-being. These techniques allow retirees to release physical and mental tension, helping them feel more balanced throughout the day (Toussaint et al., 2021).

How Physical Self-Care Can Prevent Injury and Maintain Mobility During Retirement Years

One of the most important benefits of physical self-care is its ability to **prevent injury** and **maintain mobility** as we age. As the body gets older, muscles and joints can become less flexible, and bones may lose density, making it more likely for retirees to experience falls or injuries. However, by focusing on gentle physical activities, stretching, and proper nutrition, retirees can maintain their strength, balance, and flexibility, which are key components in avoiding injury (National Institute on Aging, 2020).

Regular exercise helps to build muscle strength, which in turn supports the joints and bones, reducing the likelihood of injury from everyday movements. For example, activities like walking or swimming not only improve cardiovascular health but also help to keep the legs strong, which is crucial for maintaining balance and preventing falls. **Stretching** keeps the muscles flexible and ready to move, reducing the risk of strains or sprains (Geneen et al., 2017).

Additionally, taking care of the body through **hydration** and **nutrition** supports **bone health**. Drinking enough water helps keep the joints lubricated, while a diet rich in calcium and vitamin D can prevent the development of osteoporosis, a condition that weakens bones and makes them more prone to fractures. By paying attention to these aspects of physical health, retirees can enjoy greater mobility and independence in their day-to-day lives (National Institute of Arthritis and Musculoskeletal and Skin Diseases, 2023).

Incorporating practices like **massages** or regular **stretching routines** can also help prevent the buildup of muscle tension that might otherwise lead to discomfort or injury. Keeping the body relaxed and flexible ensures that retirees can move comfortably and enjoy the activities they love without the fear of overexertion or injury.

Managing Stress in Retirement

Retirement is a milestone many people look forward to for years, often envisioning it as a period filled with relaxation, freedom, and time to pursue passions that may have been pushed aside during their working years. However, as exciting as the prospect of retirement might be, it is also a time of immense change. This transition from the structured life of work to the open-ended days of retirement can, in some cases, be a source of significant stress. Adjusting to a new lifestyle, finding purpose outside of a career, and coping with financial or health-related concerns are just a few challenges retirees might face.

Identifying Stressors in Your Post-Work Life

For many, the idea of leaving behind the daily grind of work is something to look forward to. However, the reality of retirement can be quite different from the idyllic picture painted in our minds. One of the main challenges is adjusting to a new routine—or, for some, the lack of one. During a working career, there is usually a set structure to the day: waking up at a certain time, commuting to work, and staying busy with tasks and projects. Once this routine disappears, retirees are suddenly faced with the daunting question of how to fill their time.

The loss of daily structure can leave retirees feeling a bit disoriented or aimless. Without a schedule to follow, days can blend into one another, and it's easy to feel unproductive or even guilty for not "doing enough." This shift can be more stressful than expected, as it often requires rethinking how to spend one's time in a meaningful way.

Another major stressor during retirement is the sense of losing one's professional identity. For many people, their job defines a large part of who they are. After retirement, questions like "Who am I if I'm no longer a teacher, doctor, or engineer?" may arise. This feeling of losing a piece of oneself can contribute to a deeper sense of unease or even a kind of mourning for the life left behind.

Other Carried-Over Stressors

In addition to the stress that stems from retirement itself, many people find that stressors from their working years don't simply disappear once they stop working. Financial worries, for instance, can easily follow a person into retirement. Even with savings and pensions, there may still be anxiety about whether the money will last, how to handle rising healthcare costs, or how to manage unexpected expenses. This concern over finances can be a significant source of stress, especially if there are major changes in lifestyle or income once regular paychecks stop.

Another stressor that often persists into retirement is family obligations. Some retirees may find themselves in the role of a caregiver, either for an aging spouse, elderly parents, or even grandchildren. While these responsibilities can bring joy and fulfillment, they can also add pressure and limit the amount of personal time a retiree has to enjoy their newfound freedom.

Finally, health concerns become more prominent as we age. With retirement comes an increased focus on physical well-being, and any health challenges—whether new or ongoing—can cause additional worry. Concerns about mobility, chronic illness, or simply the process of aging itself can weigh heavily on the mind, making it difficult to fully enjoy the retirement years.

Encouraging Self-Reflection

One of the best ways to tackle stress in retirement is to first take the time to understand what's causing it. Self-reflection can be incredibly helpful in identifying stressors, both obvious and hidden. Sometimes, we aren't fully aware of what is bothering us until we sit down and ask ourselves the right questions.

Start by considering some of the following:

- **What aspects of retirement are making me feel uneasy or anxious?** It could be the lack of structure, or it could be a deeper worry about losing a sense of purpose.
- **Do I miss the social interactions and routine that work provides?** Many retirees find that they miss their colleagues and the natural social connections that come with working.
- **Am I concerned about financial stability or unexpected expenses?** Retirement can bring a shift in financial security, which can cause underlying stress.
- **Are there family responsibilities or health concerns weighing on my mind?** Understanding whether external factors are contributing to your stress can help you manage them more effectively.

Stress Management Techniques

Once you've identified the sources of your stress, it's important to find ways to manage them effectively. Below are some techniques that have been proven to help alleviate stress, particularly during retirement.

Mindfulness Meditation

Mindfulness meditation is a practice that helps individuals focus on the present moment. This technique can be particularly helpful for retirees who are struggling with stress, as it encourages a state of awareness and calmness that can reduce feelings of anxiety or overwhelm (Behan, 2020).

Mindfulness meditation involves paying attention to the here and now—your breath, your body, your surroundings—without getting caught up in thoughts about the past or future. The goal is not to clear your mind completely but to notice your thoughts and let them pass without judgment. For beginners, it may be helpful to start with just a few minutes a day. Find a quiet place where you can sit comfortably. Close your eyes, take slow, deep breaths, and focus on your breath as it enters and leaves your body. If your mind starts to wander, simply bring your attention back to your breathing. Over time, as you practice mindfulness, you may notice that you feel more grounded, less anxious, and better equipped to handle stress (Behan, 2020).

There are plenty of resources available to help guide you in your practice. Many apps offer guided meditations for beginners, walking you through each step until you feel comfortable practicing on your own.

Progressive Muscle Relaxation

Stress often manifests physically in the body, causing tension, aches, and discomfort. Progressive muscle relaxation (PMR) is a technique that helps to relieve this tension and promote physical relaxation. PMR involves tensing and then relaxing different muscle groups in your body, working systematically from your toes to your head. As you tense each group of muscles, you hold the tension for a few seconds before releasing it, allowing the muscles to fully relax. This contrast between tension and relaxation helps to reduce physical stress and brings a sense of calm to both the body and mind (Toussaint et al., 2021b).

To practice PMR, find a quiet place where you can sit or lie down comfortably. Begin with your feet—tense the muscles for a few seconds, then slowly release the tension as you breathe out. Gradually work your way up through your legs, abdomen, chest, arms, and face, paying attention to the sensations of relaxation as you release the tension in each area. This practice can help you become more aware of where you hold stress in your body and how to release it (Toussaint et al., 2021b).

Journaling

Writing down your thoughts and feelings can be a therapeutic way to manage stress. Journaling provides a space where you can explore your emotions, clarify your thoughts, and release any pent-up tension.

You don't need to follow any specific format—just write about what's on your mind. This could include how you're feeling about retirement, any worries you have about the future, or simply reflections on your day. The act of writing can help you process emotions that may be difficult to express verbally and can offer a sense of relief.

In addition to expressing stress, you can also use journaling as a way to set goals, reflect on positive experiences, or explore new interests. This practice encourages self-awareness and can help you gain insight into your own stressors and how to manage them.

Gratitude Practices

Practicing gratitude is a simple but powerful way to shift your mindset and reduce stress. By focusing on the things you are thankful for, you can train your mind to concentrate on the positives in your life rather than dwelling on what may be causing you stress.

A helpful way to start incorporating gratitude into your daily routine is to keep a gratitude journal. Each day, write down three things you are grateful for. These don't have to be grand events—something as small as a warm cup of coffee in the morning or a pleasant conversation with a friend can make a list. Over time, practicing gratitude can change the way you perceive challenges, making it easier to manage stress (Bhatt, 2024).

Gratitude practices don't just have to be about writing, either. You can express gratitude to others by thanking them for their kindness or support, which can strengthen your relationships and further reduce feelings of isolation or stress. The simple act of recognizing what you have to be grateful for can foster a sense of contentment and inner peace.

The Importance of Routine and Purpose

Retirement often brings with it a sense of freedom—freedom from the daily grind, early morning alarms, and the pressure of work deadlines. However, while this newfound freedom can be exhilarating at first, it can also create a void in our daily lives. Without the structure that work once provided, it is common for retirees to feel adrift, and this lack of routine can sometimes lead to anxiety or a sense of restlessness. As people transition into this new phase of life, finding ways to restore structure and purpose becomes essential to maintaining emotional and mental well-being.

Building a Flexible Daily Routine

One of the most effective ways to cope with the sudden openness of time that retirement brings is to build a flexible but consistent daily routine. A routine provides a framework for the day, giving it a sense of order and predictability, which can be calming for the mind. Knowing what comes next can alleviate the anxiety that often comes with too much unstructured time. However, the key here is flexibility. Retirement is a time to enjoy life without the strict obligations that come with full-time work, so while it is helpful to have a routine, it should allow for spontaneity and freedom.

A routine doesn't have to be rigid or filled with complex activities. In fact, it can be as simple as setting regular times for meals, exercise, and social activities. For example, starting each day with a walk, followed by breakfast and some time for reading or working on a hobby, can create a rhythm that makes the day feel purposeful. Even incorporating small, everyday tasks into a routine—such as gardening in the morning or taking a short nap in the afternoon—can help bring structure to the day.

Routines also help to eliminate the need for constant decision-making, which can be mentally exhausting. When the brain doesn't have to think about what comes next, it reduces the likelihood of feeling overwhelmed. A planned routine helps smooth the transition between activities and prevents the days from feeling aimless or empty.

In addition to providing structure, routines offer a sense of accomplishment. Completing small tasks each day, such as preparing meals, exercising, or even running errands, can create a feeling of productivity. This helps reduce the anxiety that often stems from not knowing how to fill one's time after retirement.

Exploring New Hobbies and Volunteering

While building a routine can provide structure, it is equally important to fill that routine with activities that bring joy, fulfillment, and a renewed sense of purpose. Retirement offers the perfect opportunity to explore new hobbies or rekindle old passions that may have been set aside during the busy working years.

Engaging in hobbies, whether creative or physical, allows retirees to invest their time in something they enjoy. For instance, learning a new skill like painting, cooking, or playing a musical instrument can be incredibly rewarding. These activities not only keep the mind active but also offer a sense of progress and achievement. Hobbies can be a powerful way to create goals, even if they are small, and provide a sense of accomplishment that helps build self-esteem.

Volunteering is another meaningful way to regain a sense of purpose during retirement. Many retirees find that volunteering allows them to give back to their community while staying socially engaged. Whether it's helping at a local charity, mentoring young people, or working with environmental groups, volunteering offers the chance to be part of something bigger than oneself. It also provides opportunities for social interaction, which is crucial for mental health and can reduce feelings of loneliness or isolation that sometimes accompany retirement.

For those who miss the routine and challenge of work but don't want to commit to full-time employment, part-time jobs or freelance work can be a great solution. These types of engagements allow retirees to stay mentally sharp and socially connected without the stress of a 9-to-5 job. Part-time work also provides an opportunity to explore different fields or industries that may not have been possible during one's career.

Whatever the choice—whether it's picking up a hobby, volunteering, or pursuing part-time work—the key is to find activities that are personally meaningful. These engagements can help retirees maintain a sense of purpose, which is essential for emotional well-being.

Purpose as a Stress Reducer and Mood Enhancer

Having a sense of purpose is fundamental to feeling fulfilled, no matter one's age or life stage. Purpose gives life meaning, and even in retirement, having something to strive for—whether it's a hobby, a volunteer project, or simply being there for family—can significantly reduce stress and improve mood.

A purposeful life doesn't need to be about grand achievements or big plans. It can be found in the small moments of everyday life. For example, something as simple as taking care of a pet, tending to a garden, or babysitting grandchildren can provide a sense of responsibility and fulfillment. These small tasks, when done with intention, give retirees a reason to get up each morning and look forward to the day ahead.

Research shows that people with a strong sense of purpose tend to experience lower levels of stress and better mental health (Sayed et al., 2024). Purpose provides direction, which helps individuals stay focused and resilient in the face of challenges. Without it, retirees may feel lost or disconnected, which can contribute to anxiety or depression. Purpose-driven activities stimulate the mind, offer a sense of satisfaction, and can improve overall emotional well-being.

When retirees have something to focus on—whether it's an ongoing project, a regular commitment like volunteering, or even a personal goal—they experience a sense of control over their lives. This feeling of control is critical in reducing anxiety, as it helps to counteract the unpredictability or uncertainty that can sometimes come with retirement. Purpose gives retirees a reason to keep learning, growing, and staying active, which, in turn, enhances mood and emotional resilience.

Seek Support and Connection

As people retire, the transition can bring about a sense of relief from the daily demands of work, but for many, it can also lead to unexpected emotional challenges. Without the usual routines and social interactions that a job provides, retirement may leave individuals feeling isolated and disconnected. This isolation can intensify feelings of burnout, especially when combined with the loss of purpose that often accompanies leaving the workforce. While burnout is typically associated with high-stress careers, it can also manifest during retirement as people struggle to adjust to a new rhythm of life that feels unfamiliar or even overwhelming.

Social isolation can worsen burnout in significant ways. When retirees are no longer surrounded by coworkers, friends, or family on a regular basis, the lack of social interaction can heighten feelings of loneliness. This loneliness, if left unchecked, can gradually spiral into more severe emotional states like depression and anxiety. When individuals spend extended periods alone without engaging in meaningful conversations or activities, they might find themselves stuck in their thoughts, focusing on negative emotions or dwelling on their frustrations. This kind of mental isolation often leads to a sense of helplessness and can make the effects of burnout seem even more severe.

However, staying connected to others plays a crucial role in alleviating these feelings of isolation and helping retirees find relief from burnout. Humans are inherently social creatures—we thrive on interaction, whether it's through deep, meaningful conversations or just the simple pleasure of spending time with others. When you have a strong support network, you can share your thoughts and concerns, gain new perspectives, and feel understood by those who care about you. In fact, just knowing that someone is there to listen can make a world of difference.

The benefits of maintaining or building connections in retirement go beyond emotional comfort. When you engage with others, especially those who are also navigating similar life transitions, you gain the opportunity to share experiences and advice. For example, someone who has recently retired might feel lost without the routine of a 9-to-5 job, but talking to others who have gone through the same experience can provide reassurance and ideas for adapting to this new phase of life. These connections offer a sense of belonging and help retirees realize that they are not alone in their journey.

Connection also helps retirees regain a sense of purpose. After leaving the structure of full-time work, many people struggle to figure out what their new role is, both within their family and in the wider world. By staying connected—whether through family, friends, or community activities—retirees can rediscover what brings them joy and fulfillment. Volunteering, mentoring, or even participating in a hobby group can provide that sense of purpose, allowing retirees to use their skills and knowledge in meaningful ways.

Additionally, connection can be a powerful stress reliever. When retirees are able to talk about their struggles, laugh with friends, or simply enjoy the company of others, they often find that their worries feel lighter. This shared experience fosters a sense of community, which can make difficult times more manageable. By staying socially engaged, retirees can counter the isolation that contributes to burnout and replace it with feelings of joy, support, and understanding.

Building and Reconnecting With Your Support Network

For some retirees, maintaining strong social connections might be easy if they have an already established network of friends, family, or community. For others, retirement may feel like the perfect time to rebuild old relationships or seek out new ones. In either case, having a supportive network can make a significant difference in how well someone adjusts to this new chapter in life.

Family Support

Family plays an irreplaceable role in providing emotional support during the transition into retirement. Whether it's a spouse, children, or extended family members, having loved ones around can offer comfort and reassurance when the challenges of retirement become overwhelming. After years of balancing work and family life, retirees may now find themselves with more time to devote to their relationships. Fostering healthy communication with family members can create a strong foundation of emotional support that helps manage feelings of stress, anxiety, or uncertainty.

Retirement can bring changes in family dynamics. With more time at home, retirees may spend more time with their spouse or partner, which can lead to both rewarding moments and, at times, challenges. It's important to communicate openly about expectations, desires, and boundaries during this transition. Retirees should not hesitate to express their feelings about the changes they are experiencing while also making an effort to understand what their partner or other family members might be going through.

For those with adult children or grandchildren, retirement offers a great opportunity to deepen these relationships. Spending more time with family—whether that means helping out with grandchildren, planning regular family gatherings, or simply checking in with loved ones—can create a stronger sense of connection. Regular communication with family helps retirees feel more involved in their loved ones' lives, which can combat feelings of loneliness or irrelevance that sometimes arise after leaving the workforce.

If relationships with family members have been strained or distant, retirement might also provide a chance to heal and reconnect. Sometimes, busy schedules and misunderstandings from the past can create emotional distance, but taking the time to reach out and rebuild those bonds can offer significant emotional rewards. Simply sharing time together or engaging in open, honest conversations can go a long way in strengthening family ties and providing a renewed sense of connection.

Friendships in Retirement

While family is often a primary source of support, friendships are just as crucial in providing emotional balance and companionship during retirement. Unlike family, friendships are relationships that people choose, which can make them especially fulfilling. However, with the busy nature of work life, many retirees might find that their friendships have faded over time. Retirement presents the perfect opportunity to rekindle old friendships and even form new ones.

To start, reaching out to old friends can bring about a sense of familiarity and comfort. Sometimes, all it takes is a phone call or a simple message to reconnect with someone who may have been a significant part of your life in the past. Setting up regular coffee dates or lunch outings can help rebuild those bonds. It's surprising how quickly the warmth of a friendship can return, even if you've been out of touch for a while.

If rekindling past friendships isn't feasible, retirement also opens the door to forming new relationships. Joining groups or participating in activities that align with personal interests is a great way to meet like-minded individuals. Whether it's a book club, a local walking group, or a gardening class, these social settings offer a chance to engage with others who share common hobbies.

For those who prefer more casual or less structured social environments, even joining a gym or taking regular walks in the neighborhood can lead to spontaneous interactions with others. Often, these informal connections can grow into meaningful friendships over time.

Moreover, many retirees are now using digital platforms to stay connected. Social media or online communities focused on specific interests can be a valuable resource for retirees who want to connect with others without leaving home. This is particularly helpful for those who may face mobility challenges or live in areas where in-person social opportunities are limited.

Community Involvement

In addition to personal relationships with family and friends, community involvement can be an incredibly fulfilling way to stay connected in retirement. Engaging with the local community not only provides opportunities to meet new people but also gives retirees a renewed sense of purpose. Many retirees find that giving back to others helps them combat feelings of isolation or burnout, as it allows them to make a positive impact in their surroundings.

Volunteering is a wonderful way to contribute while also building social connections. Whether it's at a local food bank, animal shelter, or school, volunteering allows retirees to meet people from various walks of life while contributing to causes they care about. The relationships formed through volunteer work can be deeply rewarding, as they are often built on a shared passion for helping others.

Beyond volunteering, joining local groups or clubs that focus on hobbies and interests can help retirees stay socially engaged. Many communities offer clubs centered around activities like gardening, hiking, or even photography. These groups provide an outlet for retirees to pursue their passions while making new friends. Additionally, regular group meetings can offer structure and consistency, which can be helpful for those adjusting to the open-ended nature of retirement life.

Religious or faith-based communities can also be an essential source of support for many retirees. Participation in spiritual activities, whether through attending services or getting involved in community outreach programs, helps retirees stay connected to others who share their values. Faith-based communities often offer a strong sense of belonging and purpose, which can be especially comforting during times of transition.

For retirees who enjoy learning, many communities offer lifelong learning programs where participants can take courses on a variety of topics. Whether it's a cooking class, a lecture on history, or a workshop on financial planning, these programs provide not only intellectual stimulation but also the chance to meet others with similar interests.

Seeking Professional Support

Retirement is often seen as a time of relaxation and enjoyment, but for many, it can bring unexpected challenges. Feelings of burnout, anxiety, or depression might surface as retirees adjust to their new lives. While some people may find relief through personal reflection or by reaching out to friends and family, there are times when professional guidance becomes necessary. Seeking help from therapists, counselors, or life coaches can provide retirees with the tools they need to navigate this emotional landscape and help them find a healthy balance.

When to Seek Professional Guidance

It is important to recognize that seeking professional support is not a sign of weakness; rather, it is a proactive step toward emotional well-being. Often, people might feel like they should be able to handle their problems on their own or think their struggles are not serious enough to warrant professional help. However, burnout, especially in retirement, can affect a person's mental and physical health, making it essential to seek guidance when these feelings become overwhelming.

There are several indicators that it may be time to talk to a professional. If you are finding it difficult to enjoy the activities that once brought you happiness, or if you feel persistently tired or drained despite not working, these may be signs of burnout. Additionally, feelings of hopelessness, restlessness, or irritability might indicate deeper emotional issues, such as anxiety or depression. When these emotions start interfering with daily life—making it hard to connect with loved ones, sleep well, or engage in normal routines—it is important to consider seeking support from a trained expert.

Therapists and counselors can help you work through complex emotions by providing a safe space to explore what you are feeling. Many people experience a sense of loss when they retire as they transition from a busy work life to a slower pace. For some, this loss of routine and purpose can lead to a deep sense of disorientation. A therapist or counselor can help retirees explore these emotions, unpack the changes they are experiencing, and develop new coping strategies to manage stress.

On the other hand, a life coach might be a good option for those who are struggling with finding a new direction in retirement. Life coaches often help individuals identify their goals, establish a sense of purpose, and create actionable plans to bring structure and fulfillment back into their lives. Unlike therapy, which focuses more on healing from emotional struggles, coaching tends to be more forward-looking, helping retirees focus on building a rewarding future.

Benefits of Joining Support Groups

In addition to one-on-one professional guidance, many retirees find comfort in joining support groups, particularly those centered around common struggles like burnout, anxiety, or depression. Support groups can be incredibly valuable because they provide a sense of community and belonging. When individuals come together to share their experiences, they often find comfort in knowing they are not alone in what they are going through.

One of the most significant benefits of support groups is the opportunity to connect with others who truly understand your challenges. Many retirees face similar struggles, whether it's dealing with the emotional weight of leaving a long-term career, adjusting to a new daily routine, or coping with feelings of isolation. In a support group, people can share their stories, offer advice, and listen to others in a non-judgmental environment. These interactions can be particularly uplifting, as they remind participants that their experiences are valid and that many others are navigating similar emotional journeys.

Support groups also encourage the exchange of coping strategies. Hearing how others manage their feelings of burnout or anxiety can provide practical ideas for dealing with your own stress. Whether it's learning new relaxation techniques, finding activities that bring joy, or simply having someone to talk to during difficult times, support groups can be an invaluable resource for emotional well-being.

For retirees who prefer a more structured approach, there are also support groups led by mental health professionals. These groups offer a blend of peer support and professional guidance, helping participants address their emotional challenges while benefiting from the expertise of a trained facilitator. These groups might focus on specific topics like mindfulness, grief recovery, or managing depression, and they often provide a safe space for individuals to explore their emotions in depth.

Encouraging Open Conversations With Healthcare Providers

Sometimes, people may not realize the full impact that burnout can have on their overall health and well-being. It's important to remember that emotional struggles do not just stay in the mind—they can affect the body as well. Chronic stress, anxiety, or depression can lead to physical symptoms such as headaches, fatigue, high blood pressure, or even a weakened immune system (Salleh, 2018). That is why it is essential for retirees to have open and honest conversations with their healthcare providers about how they are feeling emotionally and physically.

Many people may feel hesitant to bring up topics like burnout or anxiety with their doctors, especially if they are not used to discussing mental health. However, healthcare providers are trained to address both the physical and emotional aspects of health and can offer valuable insights and resources. By sharing how you are feeling with your doctor, you can help them better understand your overall health and ensure you are receiving comprehensive care.

For instance, if you are feeling persistently tired or lacking energy, it could be related to stress or burnout, but it might also be tied to a physical condition like a sleep disorder or nutritional deficiency. By discussing these symptoms with your doctor, you can work together to pinpoint the root cause and find appropriate treatments. Similarly, if anxiety is affecting your ability to sleep or causing physical tension, your doctor can recommend therapies or medications that might help.

Healthcare providers can also direct retirees to mental health resources, such as therapy, counseling, or support groups, depending on the individual's needs. In many cases, a doctor's referral can make it easier to access specialized care. Furthermore, doctors may recommend lifestyle changes that can improve both physical and mental well-being, such as incorporating more physical activity, practicing mindfulness, or adjusting diet and sleep patterns.

Another important aspect of talking to healthcare providers about burnout is the opportunity to address any stigmas or misconceptions that might exist around mental health care. Many people still hesitate to seek help for emotional struggles, fearing that it reflects poorly on their strength or resilience. However, by normalizing these conversations with healthcare professionals, retirees can gain a better understanding of how common these experiences are and how important it is to take action when needed.

It's Okay to Not Work Hard Anymore

For many people, especially those who have spent decades dedicated to their careers, retirement can feel both liberating and unsettling. Society has long taught us that our value is often measured by how much we achieve. From the early days of our working lives, we're told that success is built on hard work, meeting goals, and constantly staying productive. This mindset can stay with us, sometimes so deeply ingrained that it becomes part of our identity. After years of hearing phrases like "Keep pushing" or "You can rest once the job's done," it's no wonder that stepping away from work can feel disorienting.

The idea of being productive is often tied closely to self-worth. Whether we realize it or not, the jobs we do, the tasks we complete, and even the to-do lists we cross off can give us a sense of purpose. Society tends to applaud those who are always busy and always achieving, and as a result, many of us have learned to tie our value to what we accomplish. But what happens when you retire and that work is no longer part of your daily routine? The shift from constant activity to a more relaxed lifestyle can leave retirees feeling unsure of themselves, even though this is supposed to be a time of rest and enjoyment.

It's important to recognize that this pressure to be productive doesn't just disappear with retirement. Even after years of hard work, it can be challenging to suddenly let go of the feeling that every moment needs to be filled with doing something "worthwhile." But here's the thing—retirement offers the perfect opportunity to step back and redefine what "worthwhile" really means. It's not about what you produce anymore; it's about how you feel and how you choose to spend your time.

This is where the shift from "doing" to "being" becomes so essential. You don't have to constantly check off tasks to prove your value. Instead, try focusing on the joy of simply being present. Maybe it's sitting quietly with a cup of coffee in the morning, watching the sunrise without any rush to start a busy day. Maybe it's spending time with your grandchildren, going on a peaceful walk, or reading a book for no other reason than pure enjoyment. These moments, though they may not feel "productive" in the traditional sense, are just as valuable, if not more so, in this new stage of life.

For those who have always measured success by how much they achieve, slowing down can feel like a challenge. The idea that it's okay to relax might even seem foreign. But it's important to remember that after decades of hard work, you have earned this time. You don't have to push yourself to stay as active or busy as you were before. Letting go of the need to work hard every day is not only okay — it's necessary for your well-being.

Embracing This Phase of Life

Once you begin to let go of the need to constantly be doing, the next step is to embrace this new phase of life. Retirement is often seen as the end of something—the end of work, the end of responsibilities. But in reality, it's the beginning of a new chapter, one that is meant to be enjoyed at a much slower pace. This is a time to rest, and rest is not just a luxury—it's a necessity, especially after years of balancing work, family, and other commitments.

The beauty of resting at this stage of life lies in the fact that you no longer have to justify it. You don't need to feel guilty for taking things slow or for spending time simply relaxing. Whether it's an afternoon nap, a leisurely walk, or even a day spent doing absolutely nothing, rest is something you deserve. It's not about being lazy or unproductive; it's about recognizing that this is your time to recharge and enjoy life without the pressure to constantly be on the move.

However, it's also important to acknowledge that adjusting to this new pace may not always be easy. For many, retirement can bring up feelings of loss—not just the loss of a job, but the loss of a sense of purpose. Work often provides structure and identity, so when it's no longer part of your life, it's natural to feel a bit adrift. These emotions are completely normal and understandable. There's nothing wrong with missing the routine or feeling unsure of what comes next.

But retirement also offers a chance to redefine what purpose means for you. Just because you're no longer working doesn't mean you can't find meaning in other areas of life. Maybe you discover that you have more time to spend with loved ones, or perhaps you take up a hobby that you've always wanted to try. Some retirees find fulfillment in volunteering, while others enjoy spending their days outdoors, gardening, or traveling. The point is that your purpose doesn't have to be tied to a career. It can be found in the small joys of everyday life.

As you settle into this new phase, it's also important to confront and release any feelings of guilt. It's common for retirees to struggle with guilt—guilt over not working anymore, guilt over not being as "productive" as they once were. But here's the truth: you've spent years contributing through your work, and now is the time to give yourself permission to relax without feeling like you're letting anyone down.

One way to start releasing this guilt is by challenging the thoughts that cause it. When you catch yourself feeling guilty for not being as active or busy as before, remind yourself that this is your time to rest. You don't owe anyone an explanation for taking things easy. In fact, you deserve it after all the years of hard work. Retirement isn't about living up to anyone's expectations but your own. You've earned the right to enjoy this chapter at your own pace.

Another helpful step in reframing guilt is to practice mindfulness. Focus on being present in the moment, whether that moment is spent resting, walking, or even daydreaming. By staying grounded in the present, you can begin to appreciate the joy in simply being, without the pressure of having to constantly do something. Mindfulness can help shift your focus from productivity to peace, reminding you that life is just as meaningful when you take the time to savor it.

It's also essential to surround yourself with supportive people. Share your feelings of guilt or uncertainty with loved ones who understand what you're going through. Chances are, they will remind you that your worth is not measured by how much you do but by who you are. Your family and friends love you for the person you are, not for how much you achieve. This support can be a powerful reminder that your value isn't tied to productivity, and it can help you feel more comfortable embracing rest without guilt.

In conclusion, it's okay—and necessary—to not work hard anymore. After years of dedicating yourself to your career and responsibilities, retirement is a time to shift your focus from productivity to well-being. It's a time to rest, to slow down, and to enjoy the moments that may have once seemed insignificant but are now the essence of your days. Give yourself the gift of permission to relax, knowing that you've earned every bit of it. Life after work is not about how much you do but about how deeply you enjoy the life you've worked so hard to create.

Chapter 5:

New Interests or Hobbies?

Why Not?

Retirement often comes with a common piece of advice that most people have probably heard at least once: "Now's the time to find a new hobby!" While this suggestion is usually given with the best of intentions, it can feel a bit overwhelming for many. There's an expectation, almost unspoken, that as soon as retirement begins, people should start enjoying activities like quilting, fishing, or gardening just because those seem to be the stereotypical retirement pastimes. And, well, it's not surprising if that pressure to dive into these traditional hobbies doesn't feel quite right for everyone. After all, not everyone finds joy in the same things, and that's perfectly fine.

The real beauty of retirement lies in the freedom to explore—without any pressure—to find what truly brings joy and fulfillment. It's a wonderful opportunity to reconnect with old passions, discover new interests, or even just enjoy moments of leisure without feeling like you have to live up to any particular standard. The excitement doesn't have to come from the typical activities that we associate with retirement. Instead, it can come from anything that sparks your personal interest, whether it's something you used to love doing or something you've never tried before but always wanted to.

One of the most important things to remember is that it's not about following a set path that society expects. Instead, this stage of life can be approached with an open mind, ready to explore whatever feels right for you. It could be that you find joy in something that brought you happiness in your younger years, or maybe there's a hobby you never really had time to pursue during your busy working life.

Whatever it is, retirement offers the perfect opportunity to dive in without any of the time constraints you might have faced before.

The key here isn't to rush into finding a new hobby or to feel like you need to check certain boxes. Rather, it's about giving yourself the space to discover what makes you feel most content. You might find yourself gravitating toward activities that reconnect you with who you were as a child, like riding bikes or painting, or perhaps something that you only had time for on rare occasions during your working years, like reading a good book in a quiet coffee shop. The possibilities are as open as your imagination allows, and with the right mindset, retirement can be the start of a new and exciting chapter full of discovery and enjoyment.

Rediscovering Old Passions After Retirement

For years, work schedules and responsibilities may have taken center stage, leaving little room for personal interests. But now, with more free time, there's a wonderful opportunity to reconnect with old passions and rediscover those things that once brought you joy. This can be a truly transformative experience, allowing you to tap into parts of yourself that might have been set aside for decades.

Revisiting old hobbies can be like finding a piece of yourself that's been missing, and it opens the door to new possibilities. Whether it's something you cherished as a child or a passion that remained hidden during your working years, reconnecting with these interests can bring a deep sense of fulfillment, purpose, and happiness. The beauty of this stage of life is that you now have the time and freedom to truly immerse yourself in these activities without the distractions of a career or other demands pulling you away.

Childhood Revisited

Let's take a moment to go back to your childhood. What were the things that filled your days with laughter and excitement? Maybe it was the freedom of riding your bike around the neighborhood, the thrill of racing down the street with friends by your side. You might even remember the simple joy of picking flowers in a nearby field, admiring their colors and fragrances. These memories, while perhaps long-forgotten, often hold the key to the kind of happiness that we lose track of as we grow older.

Reconnecting with these childhood activities in retirement can be like stepping into a time machine that takes you back to a more carefree, joyful version of yourself. When you were a child, everything felt possible, and there was no pressure to be perfect or to compete with others. You just did what you loved because it made you happy. For instance, picking up that old bike again could reignite a sense of adventure that you haven't felt in years. Imagine the wind brushing against your face as you cycle down a quiet road, not for exercise or to run errands, but just for the pure fun of it.

Perhaps you loved spending time outdoors, running through fields, or climbing trees. That connection to nature can still bring peace and contentment in retirement. A walk through a local park or even spending time in your garden can bring back the same feelings of wonder you had as a child. And because you're not rushing off to meetings or obligations, you can fully enjoy the experience, savoring the little details you might have missed before.

Hidden Hobbies of Adulthood

As we grow older and take on more responsibilities, our days fill up quickly. Jobs, families, and various commitments often leave little room for personal hobbies. But even during those busy years, many of us managed to squeeze in a few moments here and there for activities we enjoyed. Maybe you spent occasional weekends swimming at a local pool or used those rare quiet afternoons to sit in a coffee shop with a good book. These hidden hobbies, though tucked away for long stretches of time, are a reflection of your true passions, and they can be rediscovered in retirement.

Think about how it felt to carve out a little time for yourself in the middle of a hectic schedule. Maybe you loved swimming, feeling the calmness of the water as you glided through the pool, or the weightlessness that helped melt away the stress of the workweek. Now that you have more time, swimming can become a regular part of your routine, not just an occasional escape. The physical benefits are certainly a bonus, but the real joy comes from doing something that makes you feel alive, at peace, and connected to yourself.

Or perhaps it was those peaceful moments spent in a cozy corner of your favorite coffee shop, reading a novel or writing in a journal. The hustle and bustle of life often limited how often you could indulge in this small luxury. But in retirement, you can bring this hobby back into your life, spending lazy afternoons reading or writing without worrying about deadlines or errands. These simple pleasures are more than just pastimes; they're opportunities to slow down and enjoy life in a way that you couldn't before. You'll find that these hobbies, once hidden by the demands of adulthood, can now take center stage, enriching your days and giving you something to look forward to.

Inspirations From Recent Years

In the years leading up to retirement, it's not uncommon to feel sparks of interest in new activities, but time often isn't on your side to explore them. Maybe you've always wanted to take up writing but never had the chance to fully dive into it. Or maybe there's been an idea bubbling in your mind for years—something creative, like inventing or crafting—that you've been itching to try but just couldn't fit into your busy life. Retirement is the perfect opportunity to explore these newfound passions, and there's something incredibly exciting about embarking on a journey of discovery with no pressure and no rush.

For some, writing becomes a powerful way to express thoughts, emotions, and ideas that have been waiting to come out. You might have kept a journal during your working years or jotted down ideas for stories, but now you can fully commit to this passion. Writing allows you to reflect on your experiences, share your stories with others, or simply enjoy the process of putting your thoughts into words. It's a deeply personal activity, one that can be both rewarding and therapeutic.

Others may feel drawn to more hands-on, inventive pursuits. Maybe you've had ideas for projects or inventions but never had the time or energy to explore them fully. In retirement, you have the freedom to play around with these ideas, experiment, and see where your creativity takes you. The best part is that there's no need for perfection—just the excitement of trying something new and watching it come to life.

The retirement phase can also bring uncertainty. Without the familiar rhythm of work, it's easy to settle into routines that feel safe and predictable. While comfort is important, staying too long in these comfort zones can lead to feelings of stagnation. To truly embrace the richness that retirement offers, it's essential to step outside these boundaries and embrace new experiences.

By doing so, life remains exciting, full of discovery, and deeply fulfilling. Whether it's trying a new hobby, joining a club, or venturing into a new part of the world, stepping out of the familiar brings both challenges and rewards. And the truth is, the most rewarding moments often come when we dare to push ourselves beyond the usual.

Joining New Circles

One of the most refreshing ways to step out of your comfort zone after retirement is by expanding your social horizons. Many people, after retiring, find that the social interactions they once took for granted. However, this doesn't mean your social life has to diminish. In fact, retirement offers the perfect opportunity to explore new social circles that align with your current or emerging interests.

Think about joining a club that focuses on something you've always been curious about, like a photography group, a gardening club, or a hiking society. You may have loved photography for years, snapping pictures here and there, but joining a group of fellow enthusiasts can take this hobby to the next level. Meeting people who share your interests not only broadens your skills but also connects you with a community of like-minded individuals. You suddenly have a group of people who motivate you to get out there, experiment with new techniques, and explore your surroundings in ways you never did before.

Take gardening, for example. It's about learning from others, sharing tips, and even participating in community projects like beautifying local parks or contributing to community gardens. These social circles become more than just a pastime; they offer a chance to deepen your engagement with the things you love while simultaneously pushing you to try new things.

And it doesn't stop there. Trying something completely unfamiliar, like salsa dancing or joining a theater group, could open doors to experiences you never imagined. You might find yourself meeting people who broaden your worldview and expose you to perspectives that challenge and inspire you. The beauty of joining new circles is that it keeps you engaged with life, offering a sense of belonging and community that continues to enrich your retirement years.

Educational Ventures

While retirement is often thought of as a time to slow down, it's also a fantastic time to dive into learning—this time, purely for the joy of it. Educational ventures, whether in the form of workshops, seminars, or online courses, offer a unique way to step out of your comfort zone and broaden your horizons. And the best part is, there are no grades, no pressure—just the pure pleasure of learning something new.

You may have always been interested in a subject but never had the time to explore it fully. Now, with more time on your hands, you could sign up for an online course on history, photography, or even a foreign language. Imagine brushing up on French, not because you need it for work but simply because you've always wanted to converse in another language or immerse yourself in another culture. Picture yourself attending a local workshop on pottery or painting, where the focus is not on perfection but on enjoying the creative process. These educational experiences give you the chance to stretch your mind in ways that are both fun and stimulating.

Learning alongside others brings a shared sense of purpose. The energy that comes from group learning is infectious—you'll feel motivated, curious, and maybe even a little out of your depth at first. But that's the joy of stepping out of your comfort zone—you're challenging yourself, and with each step forward, you're opening up a world of possibilities.

Theme-Based Vacations

One of the most exciting ways to step out of your comfort zone in retirement is by transforming your vacations into immersive experiences based on your newfound or lifelong interests. Instead of sticking to the usual beach holiday or city break, why not plan a trip that revolves around something you've always wanted to explore in greater depth? The idea of a theme-based vacation takes travel to a whole new level, allowing you to combine relaxation with the thrill of discovering something new.

For example, if you've developed an interest in history, you could plan a vacation that takes you on guided tours of ancient cities, historical landmarks, or famous battlefields. Imagine walking through the ruins of Rome or visiting the castles of Scotland with a knowledgeable guide who brings the history to life. Each day of your trip becomes an opportunity to learn and immerse yourself in the stories of the past, all while exploring new places.

Or maybe you've taken up photography as a hobby. A nature photography tour could be the perfect way to not only improve your skills but also see the world through a new lens—literally. Imagine traveling to the mountains of Patagonia or the rolling hills of Tuscany, capturing the landscapes, wildlife, and local culture as part of your adventure. These theme-based vacations push you to engage more deeply with your interests while experiencing the beauty of travel in a unique and purposeful way.

For some, culinary tours might inspire you. You could plan a vacation around exploring the cuisines of different countries, attending cooking classes, and learning to prepare traditional dishes from local chefs. These trips are about more than just sightseeing—they offer a fully immersive experience that makes each day of travel exciting and deeply rewarding.

Volunteer Work

Another deeply fulfilling way to step out of your comfort zone in retirement is through volunteer work. Volunteering is not only a way to give back to your community, but it also allows you to explore new interests and discover talents you might not have realized you had. For example, if you've always enjoyed reading, you could volunteer at a local library or school, reading to children and fostering a love of books in the next generation. Imagine sitting in a cozy reading nook with a group of kids, their eyes wide with wonder as you bring the characters and stories to life. It's an experience that not only helps them but also gives them a sense of purpose and connection to their community.

Or maybe you've developed an interest in gardening or sustainability. Volunteering at a community garden can offer you the chance to dig in literally while contributing to a project that benefits others. Community gardens often need helping hands to grow food for local food banks or beautify public spaces, and your involvement can make a visible difference. It's a great way to spend time outdoors, meet new people, and use your skills for the greater good.

Even more rewarding is the fact that volunteering can take you to places you've never been before—both literally and figuratively. You might find yourself working alongside people from all walks of life, learning from their experiences, and discovering new perspectives. Volunteering pushes you out of your comfort zone in the best possible way, allowing you to grow and contribute while staying active and engaged.

Embracing and Enjoying Leisure After Retirement

Retirement is a chance to explore hobbies and activities simply for the joy they bring, without the pressure to be productive or achieve something measurable. Instead of viewing free time through the lens of accomplishments, retirement allows you to savor each moment for what it is—a time to relax, engage with your passions, and discover new interests.

One of the most fulfilling aspects of leisure in retirement is that it doesn't have to be tied to any sense of obligation. There's no need to turn hobbies into work, no requirement to excel, and no pressure to stay productive. This time is yours, and it's perfectly okay to engage in activities just for the sheer enjoyment of them.

Casual Exploration

The beauty of casual exploration lies in its freedom—you can dip your toes into various interests without feeling any pressure to commit or excel. This is a wonderful way to discover new sources of joy that you may not have encountered during your working years.

In retirement, you can spend a weekend taking photos at a nearby park just to see if it's something you enjoy. There's no pressure to capture the perfect shot or master the latest techniques. You're simply allowing yourself the space to try something new. If you like it, great! And if not, that's okay too—there are countless other hobbies waiting to be explored.

Think of casual exploration as a playground for your curiosity. You might take a cooking class one week, try your hand at watercolor painting the next, or even join a yoga group just to see what it's like. The point isn't to become an expert at any of these things but to enjoy the experience of learning and experimenting. It's in these moments of discovery that you might find something that brings unexpected joy into your life.

Even activities that don't seem to "click" can offer valuable insights. Let's say you take up knitting after hearing how relaxing it can be, but after a few attempts, you realize it's not for you. That's perfectly fine! The experience itself has value because it allows you to try something different. Casual exploration is about giving yourself permission to enjoy activities for what they are—a way to pass the time pleasantly, without the weight of expectations.

Joyful Continuation

For many, these long-time hobbies are a source of relaxation and stability. Picture yourself sitting in a sunlit room with your favorite book, finally able to immerse yourself in the story without the distraction of work emails or deadlines. Or maybe it's the feeling of tending to your garden, watching your plants grow and thrive, knowing you now have the time to truly nurture them. These moments offer a sense of continuity, grounding you in the things that have always been important to you.

The beauty of continuing with familiar hobbies is that they require little effort to get started again. You don't need to learn anything new—you already know how to play that piano piece you've practiced for years or bake the perfect loaf of bread. What's different now is that you have to savor these activities without rushing through them. You can take pleasure in the process, whether it's spending a quiet afternoon knitting or indulging in a full day of birdwatching in the park.

Continuing with these hobbies also provides a sense of accomplishment, but not in the pressured way that work might have demanded. Instead, it's about personal satisfaction—doing something well simply because it makes you happy. These activities become a cherished part of your routine, offering comfort and joy as you navigate this new chapter of life.

Letting Go of Non-Joyous Activities

One of the greatest freedoms that comes with retirement is the ability to let go of activities that no longer bring you joy. During your working years, you may have felt obligated to stick with certain hobbies or commitments out of a sense of duty or because they fit into your limited schedule. But retirement opens the door to reevaluating how you spend your time, and that includes the power to say no to things that don't make you happy.

Perhaps you once enjoyed tennis, but now the thought of playing feels more like a chore than a delight. Or maybe you joined a community group that no longer sparks your interest, but you've kept attending out of habit. Retirement offers the perfect opportunity to step back and ask yourself, "Does this still bring me joy?" If the answer is no, there's no need to continue. Letting go of non-joyous activities is not about giving up—it's about recognizing that your time is valuable and should be spent on things that truly uplift and energize you.

By freeing yourself from activities that no longer serve you, you create space for new experiences or more time for the hobbies you genuinely enjoy. It's a liberating feeling to realize that you have full control over how you fill your days. There's no need to stick with something just because you've always done it. In fact, letting go can often lead to a sense of renewal as you open yourself up to new possibilities that align with your current interests and passions.

Think of it this way: retirement is your time to prioritize what brings you joy. If an activity feels like an obligation or doesn't light you up the way it once did, it's okay to let it go. This process of shedding old commitments can be incredibly freeing, allowing you to focus on the activities that bring a sense of fun, relaxation, and fulfillment into your life.

Life's Little Interests

When we're caught up in the busyness of work and family, we often overlook the small pleasures of life—the quiet moments and the simple things that can spark joy. One of the most rewarding aspects of retirement is the opportunity to slow down and notice life's little details. These small moments, when viewed with curiosity, can lead to a renewed sense of interest and excitement. Retirement gives you the chance to reconnect with the world around you in a way that may have been difficult before.

For example, something as simple as spending time in your garden or noticing the birds chirping outside your window can spark a new interest in birdwatching or gardening. Imagine sitting in your backyard one afternoon, with no particular plans or appointments to rush off to, and noticing the different species of birds that visit your trees. One moment, you're sipping a cup of tea, and the next, you're wondering about the names and behaviors of these feathered visitors. Perhaps that curiosity leads you to pick up a book on local bird species, or maybe it inspires you to visit a nearby nature reserve. What starts as a casual observation can evolve into a fulfilling hobby.

Similarly, walking through a park could make you appreciate the variety of plants, trees, and flowers that surround you. It's not uncommon for retirees to rediscover a love for nature simply because they now have the time to notice its beauty. From taking up photography to capturing the colors of the changing seasons to sketching the landscape or learning the basics of botany, life's little interests are all around, just waiting to be explored. These small moments of curiosity can become the seeds for much larger discoveries.

One retiree I spoke to once shared how she stumbled upon knitting purely by accident. She had never considered herself particularly crafty, but one day, while attending a local market, she noticed a booth selling beautiful, hand-knitted scarves and sweaters. It sparked her curiosity, and she decided to give it a try. What began as a small interest grew into a full-blown passion for knitting, and now she even teaches classes at her local community center. Life's little interests, when nurtured, can take you down paths you never expected.

Starting Small

The thought of diving headfirst into a new hobby or interest can sometimes feel overwhelming, especially for those who have spent most of their lives focused on a specific career or raising a family. Many retirees worry that they don't have the skills or experience to take on something new. However, it's important to remember that no interest is too small or insignificant to explore. The key is to start small. Taking those first small steps can often lead to much bigger and more exciting explorations later on.

For instance, if you've always been interested in cooking but never had the time to experiment in the kitchen, retirement is the perfect opportunity to start. Begin with simple recipes, or maybe start by exploring one cuisine that has always intrigued you. There's no need to aim for perfection right away—just the act of trying something new can be incredibly rewarding. You might start by making a dish from a new cookbook, and before you know it, you could find yourself organizing dinner parties for friends and family or even enrolling in a cooking class. By starting small, you can build confidence and gradually expand your skills without feeling pressured to excel immediately.

Similarly, you might feel drawn to creative pursuits like painting, drawing, or photography. You don't have to produce masterpieces on your first try. In fact, many retirees find joy in simply experimenting with different materials and techniques without any expectation of perfection. One small step—such as attending a local art class or setting up a camera during a morning walk—can lead to a lifetime of discovery. The joy of starting small is that it removes the pressure to be great right away. You can allow yourself to learn, grow, and evolve at your own pace.

Another powerful example of starting small is seen in physical activities. Retirement provides an excellent opportunity to focus on wellness and health, and that could begin with something as simple as adding a short walk to your daily routine. Many retirees have found that what began as a 10-minute walk each day soon grew into a love for hiking, cycling, or even yoga. Starting small with physical activity allows you to gradually build strength, endurance, and confidence—transforming what initially seemed like a small step into a major lifestyle change that enhances both your mental and physical health.

Comfort Zone Challenges

Perhaps one of the most transformative aspects of retirement is the opportunity to step out of your comfort zone. After spending decades following routines, handling responsibilities, and often putting the needs of others first, retirement offers the perfect time to challenge yourself and try things you might never have considered before. Stepping out of your comfort zone might feel intimidating, but it is often through these experiences that we grow the most and find new avenues of happiness.

Pushing your boundaries doesn't mean you need to take on massive, life-altering challenges. It could be something as simple as joining a club or group where you don't know anyone or trying a hobby that's entirely different from anything you've done before. For example, maybe you've always admired people who can speak more than one language. Maybe learning a new language seems like an enormous task, but by taking a class or practicing with a language app, you can start small and see where it takes you. The act of stepping into the unknown, even in small ways, can be exhilarating and empowering.

One retiree shared her story of stepping out of her comfort zone by joining a salsa dancing class. She had never been much of a dancer, but something about the music and the energy of the dance intrigued her. Although she felt nervous at first, she decided to give it a try. That initial hesitation quickly turned into excitement as she made new friends, improved her dancing skills, and even started attending dance events. The experience not only boosted her confidence but also brought a new level of joy to her life. It all began with a willingness to challenge her comfort zone.

Another retiree, who had spent his career as a lawyer, found himself stepping out of his comfort zone in an entirely different way. After retiring, he joined a local theater group—something he had never imagined doing while working. At first, the thought of standing on stage in front of an audience terrified him, but he decided to give it a try. He started with a small role and gradually worked his way up to more prominent parts. He discovered that acting allowed him to express himself in ways he hadn't before, and the experience became one of the highlights of his retirement. His willingness to step out of his comfort zone led to personal growth and a newfound passion.

Stepping out of your comfort zone doesn't always have to involve big leaps; even small steps can lead to significant changes. If you've always stuck to familiar activities or social circles, try something new—perhaps join a book club, take a painting class, or volunteer for a cause that speaks to you. The sense of accomplishment that comes from trying something different is often enough to inspire you to continue exploring and pushing the boundaries of what you thought was possible.

Learning From Others

One of the most comforting things about entering retirement is knowing that you are not alone in this transition. Many others are navigating the same life changes, and talking to peers who are also figuring out their new routines can be a source of invaluable support. Conversations with other retirees often lead to a shared exchange of ideas, experiences, and advice that can help you make the most of your free time.

When you engage with others in the same stage of life, you quickly discover that everyone has their own unique approach to filling their retirement years. Some people might share stories of how they've reignited old passions, like playing an instrument they haven't touched in decades. Others may talk about new hobbies they've taken up, such as painting, pottery, or gardening. These conversations can spark inspiration. You might hear about a local group that gathers for early morning hikes or a knitting club that meets every week, and suddenly, a new possibility for your own time opens up.

It's worth remembering that many retirees feel uncertain about how to navigate this chapter of life. In fact, sharing your own experiences—both the highs and the challenges—can help create a sense of solidarity among your peers. Whether you're talking to someone over a cup of coffee or chatting in a casual gathering at a community center, these interactions help ease the sometimes difficult emotions that come with such a major life shift. Listening to how others manage their days, handle the new dynamics of their relationships, or stay active in their communities offers perspective and can help alleviate the pressure of feeling like you need to have everything figured out from day one.

Talking to others also helps retirees learn practical tips that may not have been obvious before. For instance, someone might mention a local class they've joined that's not widely advertised or suggest ways to get involved in volunteer opportunities that align with personal values. Some might even share strategies on how to manage finances better in retirement or how they've found fulfilling part-time work that keeps them engaged without the pressures of full-time employment. Learning from others becomes a rich, two-way street—an exchange of ideas that broadens your horizons and enriches your experience of retirement.

Joining Groups

While casual conversations and one-on-one interactions are helpful, there's also something incredibly powerful about becoming part of a formal group or organization. Joining a group—whether it's a hobby-based club, a volunteer organization, or a fitness class—provides retirees with a structured way to engage with their interests and the wider community. The social support offered by these groups plays a vital role in promoting mental and emotional well-being, especially for those adjusting to the new dynamics of post-retirement life.

For many retirees, joining a group brings a sense of routine and purpose back into daily life. It provides a reason to get out of the house, meet new people, and invest time in an activity that brings joy or satisfaction. For instance, if you've always loved photography but never had the time to pursue it seriously, joining a photography club gives you the chance to not only improve your skills but also meet people who share the same passion. Learning from others in a group setting adds a whole new dimension to the experience—members often share tips, offer feedback, and celebrate each other's growth.

Group settings also provide a built-in support system. In these environments, you meet people who are at various stages of their own retirement journey, and you quickly realize that everyone brings something valuable to the table. Some members might be seasoned pros at the activity you're learning, while others are complete beginners. This diversity of experience fosters an atmosphere of encouragement rather than competition, and it allows everyone to grow together.

Take, for example, fitness groups like yoga classes or walking clubs. These offer not only physical benefits but also social ones. A weekly yoga class can become much more than just a way to stay fit—it can turn into a social event where you chat with classmates before and after sessions, sharing stories about life, health, and even challenges in adapting to retirement. Over time, these interactions develop into friendships that extend beyond the gym or studio.

In addition to formal clubs, there are plenty of casual meetups that retirees can join. These range from book clubs and dinner groups to travel circles that plan trips together. Whether formal or informal, these group settings allow retirees to engage in lifelong learning, an important factor in maintaining cognitive health and staying mentally sharp. Learning something new alongside others fosters a sense of accomplishment and reminds retirees that growth doesn't stop when one leaves the workforce—it merely shifts to new, often more enjoyable, pursuits.

The Power of Laughter

One of the most important things to remember is that it's not about how "good" you are at something or how quickly you master a new skill. The real key is enjoying the journey, and one of the best ways to make sure you're having fun is through laughter. Humor has a special ability to lighten the mood, reduce stress, and bring people together, making new experiences feel less daunting and far more enjoyable.

Imagine trying something new for the first time, like a dance class or a cooking workshop. At first, it might feel intimidating, especially if you're unfamiliar with the steps or you fumble your way through a recipe. But when you're surrounded by others who are equally unsure and willing to laugh at their own mistakes, it transforms the entire experience. Instead of feeling embarrassed, you find yourself laughing along with everyone else, realizing that it's perfectly okay to be imperfect. In fact, these moments of shared humor often become the most memorable parts of the experience.

Laughter also helps break the ice in group settings, particularly when you're meeting new people. Whether it's a hiking group, a painting class, or a volunteer team, humor can dissolve any initial awkwardness and pave the way for more genuine connections. A well-timed joke or a shared laugh over a mishap turns strangers into friends and makes everyone feel more at ease. Before you know it, the group starts to feel like a second family—people you look forward to seeing, not just because of the activity but because of the camaraderie and fun you share together.

Moreover, humor has real health benefits. Studies have shown that laughter can improve mood, lower blood pressure, and even boost the immune system. For retirees, staying physically healthy is important, but mental and emotional health are just as crucial. Incorporating humor into your daily activities and social interactions provides a natural way to reduce stress, lift spirits, and increase your overall sense of happiness. When laughter is part of the mix, everything feels a little lighter, and challenges that might have seemed overwhelming become more manageable.

In group settings, humor also fosters a sense of belonging. As people share stories, laugh at inside jokes, and bond over shared experiences, they develop stronger relationships. A knitting group that shares a laugh over someone's accidental knitting disaster becomes more than just a gathering—it becomes a safe, supportive space where people can be themselves without fear of judgment. These moments of shared laughter help create lasting memories and friendships, reminding retirees that life after work can still be filled with joy and connection.

Community and social integration are fundamental to a fulfilling and joyful retirement. While the transition from a career-driven life to one focused on leisure can feel uncertain at times, the connections you build with others help anchor you during this change. Talking to peers and learning from their experiences provides invaluable insights and inspiration. Joining groups or clubs offers a structured way to explore new hobbies while forming deep, lasting relationships. And never underestimate the power of laughter—it brings joy, lightens the mood, and helps turn ordinary moments into treasured memories.

Conclusion

Retirement is not the end of the road; it is the beginning of a new journey.
– Unknown

You are standing at the threshold of retirement, maybe with a mix of excitement and uncertainty swirling in your mind; it's important to take a moment to reflect on the incredible journey that has brought you here. You've spent decades dedicating yourself to your work, building a life filled with accomplishments, relationships, and memories. Now, a new chapter awaits—a chapter that holds the promise of freedom, exploration, and a different kind of fulfillment.

It's natural to feel hesitant about stepping into this next phase of life. After all, work has been a significant part of your identity for so long. The routine, the challenges, the sense of purpose—it has all shaped who you are today. But retirement doesn't mean leaving all that behind; instead, it offers an opportunity to rediscover yourself in new and exciting ways.

You've often dreamed of a life where time is your own, haven't you? A life where you can wake up without the shrill sound of an alarm clock, sip your morning coffee while watching the sunrise, and plan your day based on what brings you joy rather than what demands your attention. Now, that life is within reach. The world is out there, waiting for you to explore its wonders—from the bustling streets of cities, you've yet to visit the serene landscapes that take your breath away.

Your pension fund, the one you've diligently contributed to over the years, is ready to support this new adventure. It's more than just a financial safety net; it's a testament to your hard work, discipline, and foresight. You've earned the right to enjoy the fruits of your labor and to indulge in experiences that enrich your life and broaden your horizons. So, why not take that trip you've always talked about? Visit the places that have long been on your bucket list, and create memories that will stay with you forever.

But it's not just about travel and exploration. Retirement also offers the precious gift of time—time to spend with your loved ones in ways that might not have been possible before. Your family, who have always cherished the moments they could share with you, will welcome the chance to create new memories together. Imagine being able to attend every family gathering without worrying about work commitments or being there to support your grandchildren as they grow and discover the world around them.

For instance, think about the joy of teaching your grandchild how to ride a bike, your hands steadying them as they find their balance. Picture the laughter shared during a spontaneous picnic in the park or the warmth of family stories told around the dinner table. These are the moments that enrich our lives, moments that become the cherished memories we hold dear.

It's also important to acknowledge how far you've come and the toll that years of hard work can take. Burnout is real, and it's okay to admit that you're feeling tired. You've spent so much time meeting deadlines, handling responsibilities, and pushing through challenges that it's easy to forget the importance of rest and rejuvenation. Retirement offers you the chance to focus on your well-being, listen to your body's needs, and replenish your energy.

Consider taking up activities that nurture your mind and body. Maybe you've always wanted to try yoga or meditation, practices that can bring a sense of peace and balance to your life. Perhaps long walks in nature appeal to you, allowing you to breathe in fresh air and marvel at the beauty around you. This is your time to prioritize yourself, something that might have been difficult amidst the demands of a busy career.

Moreover, retirement opens the door to exploring new interests and hobbies. Have you ever found yourself saying, "If only I had the time, I would love to learn how to paint," or play an instrument, or perhaps even write a book? Well, now you do have the time. You can dive into these passions without the constraints of a tight schedule. It's an opportunity to discover talents you never knew you had, to challenge yourself in new ways, and to find joy in the process of learning and creating.

For example, imagine setting up an easel by a sunny window, the canvas blank and full of possibilities. As you dip your brush into vibrant colors and let your imagination guide your hand, you might find a sense of satisfaction and peace that you hadn't expected. Or picture yourself strumming a guitar, the notes slowly coming together into a melody that brings a smile to your face. These are the simple pleasures that can make each day fulfilling.

It's understandable to have concerns about the financial aspects of retirement. Adjusting to a different income can be daunting, and you might worry about maintaining your current lifestyle. However, it's important to remember that wealth isn't solely measured by monetary means. The richness of life is also found in the freedom to spend your time as you choose, in the relationships you nurture, and in the experiences that bring you happiness.

You might find that with more time, you appreciate the simpler things—like gardening, cooking, or reading—that don't require significant spending but offer immense satisfaction. Perhaps you'll discover that the reduction in work-related expenses and the stress that comes with a demanding job more than compensate for a smaller income. It's about finding a balance that allows you to live comfortably while enjoying the newfound freedom retirement brings.

As you contemplate this significant transition, take pride in all that you've achieved. Reflect on the projects you've completed, the challenges you've overcome, and the impact you've had on colleagues and clients alike. Your career has been a journey filled with accomplishments that have not only benefited you but also those around you. Now, it's time to apply that same dedication and passion to this new chapter of your life.

Embracing retirement doesn't mean letting go of who you are; it means allowing yourself to grow in new directions. It's about recognizing that your identity is multifaceted—not just defined by your profession but also by your roles as a parent, grandparent, friend, and individual with unique interests and dreams. Retirement gives you the space to explore these other facets more deeply.

If doubts still linger, consider reaching out to friends or acquaintances who have already made this transition. They can offer valuable insights and share their experiences—the challenges they faced and the joys they discovered. Hearing their stories might reassure you that while change can be unsettling, it can also lead to some of the most rewarding times of your life.

In the end, remember that retirement is a personal journey, and there's no one-size-fits-all approach. You have the freedom to shape this chapter in a way that reflects your desires and aspirations. Whether you choose to travel the world, delve into new hobbies, volunteer in your community, or simply relish the peace of unhurried days, what matters most is that it brings you happiness and fulfillment.

So, take that step forward with confidence and optimism. Trust in the foundation you've built over the years and the resilience that has carried you through various stages of life. Embrace the opportunities that await you, knowing that you are ready—even if you haven't realized it until now.

Here's to you and the incredible journey ahead. May it be filled with laughter, discovery, love, and contentment. Your story is far from over; in many ways, it's just beginning a beautiful new chapter.

References

Behan, C. (2020). The benefits of meditation and mindfulness practices during times of crisis such as COVID-19. *Irish Journal of Psychological Medicine, 37*(4), 1–8. https://doi.org/10.1017/ipm.2020.38

Bhatt, M. (2024, June 21). The beginner's guide to gratitude journaling: How to start a gratitude journal and stick with it. *Papers & Gems.* https://www.papersandgems.com/blogs/journal/the-beginners-guide-to-gratitude-journaling-how-to-start-a-gratitude-journal-and-stick-with-it?srsltid=AfmBOopBQRpZ4t28J7bAkBXWMmichnYG3rP8p7Ra9LQyACokld7ToY_E

Boyte-White, C. (2019). *Long-term vs. short-term capital gains rates—Which is more favorable?* Investopedia. https://www.investopedia.com/articles/personal-finance/101515/comparing-longterm-vs-shortterm-capital-gain-tax-rates.asp

Cheng, M. (2024). *401(k) required minimum distributions (RMDs): Avoid these 4 mistakes.* Investopedia. https://www.investopedia.com/articles/retirement/04/120604.asp

Díaz-Silveira, C., Alcover, C.-M., Burgos, F., Marcos, A., & Santed, M. A. (2020). Mindfulness versus physical exercise: Effects of two recovery strategies on mental health, stress, and immunoglobulin A during lunch breaks. A randomized controlled trial. *International Journal of Environmental Research and Public Health, 17*(8), 2839. https://doi.org/10.3390/ijerph17082839

Elliott, B. (2018, December 13). *Epsom salt: Benefits, uses, and side effects.* Healthline; Healthline Media. https://www.healthline.com/nutrition/epsom-salt-benefits-uses

Geneen, L. J., Moore, R. A., Clarke, C., Martin, D., Colvin, L. A., & Smith, B. H. (2017). *Cochrane Database of Systematic Reviews, 4(4).* https://doi.org/10.1002/14651858.cd011279.pub3

Gotter, A. (2018, April 20). *What is the 4-7-8 breathing technique?* Healthline; Healthline Media. https://www.healthline.com/health/4-7-8-breathing

Lewine, H. (2022, March 14). *The importance of stretching.* Harvard Health; Harvard Health. https://www.health.harvard.edu/staying-healthy/the-importance-of-stretching

Lovato, N., & Lack, L. (2010). The effects of napping on cognitive functioning. *Progress in Brain Research, 185,* 155–166. https://doi.org/10.1016/B978-0-444-53702-7.00009-9

Medicare Interactive. (2019). *The parts of Medicare (A, B, C, D) - Medicare interactive.* Medicare Interactive. https://www.medicareinteractive.org/get-answers/medicare-basics/medicare-coverage-overview/original-medicare

National Institute of Arthritis and Musculoskeletal and Skin Diseases. (2023, May 5). *Calcium and vitamin D: Important for bone health.* National Institute of Arthritis and Musculoskeletal and Skin Diseases. https://www.niams.nih.gov/health-topics/calcium-and-vitamin-d-important-bone-health

National Institute on Aging. (2020, November 30). *Maintaining mobility and preventing disability are key to living independently as we age.* National Institute on Aging; National Institutes of Health. https://www.nia.nih.gov/news/maintaining-mobility-and-preventing-disability-are-key-living-independently-we-age

National Institutes of Health. (2021, June). *Mindfulness for your health.* NIH News in Health. https://newsinhealth.nih.gov/2021/06/mindfulness-your-health

Needham, E. (2024, August 15). Long-term care planning: Addressing the financial risks in retirement. *Insight Wealth Strategies.* https://insight2wealth.com/blog/long-term-care-planning-addressing-the-financial-risks-in-retirement/

Robinson, S. M. (2017). Improving nutrition to support healthy ageing: What are the opportunities for intervention? *Proceedings of the Nutrition Society, 77*(3), 257–264. https://doi.org/10.1017/s0029665117004037

Rosentson, M. (2024, February 14). *Defined-benefit pension plan vs. defined-contribution plan.* Investopedia. https://www.investopedia.com/ask/answers/032415/how-does-defined-benefit-pension-plan-differ-defined-contribution-plan.asp

Salleh, M. R. (2018). Life event, stress and illness. *The Malaysian Journal of Medical Sciences: MJMS, 15*(4), 9–18.

Sayed, T., Malan, H., & Fourie, E. (2024). Exploring the associations between resilience and psychological well-being among South Africans during COVID-19. *Frontiers in Psychology, 15.* https://doi.org/10.3389/fpsyg.2024.1323466

Scott, E. (2005, December 17). *Use guided imagery for relaxation.* Verywell Mind; Verywell Mind. https://www.verywellmind.com/use-guided-imagery-for-relaxation-3144606

Scott, E. (2024, February 12). *What is body scan meditation?* Verywell Mind. https://www.verywellmind.com/body-scan-meditation-why-and-how-3144782

Toussaint, L., Nguyen, Q. A., Roettger, C., Dixon, K., Offenbächer, M., Kohls, N., Hirsch, J., & Sirois, F. (2021a). Effectiveness of progressive muscle relaxation, deep breathing, and guided imagery in promoting psychological and physiological states of relaxation. *Evidence-Based Complementary and Alternative Medicine, 2021*(1), 1–8. https://doi.org/10.1155/2021/5924040

Toussaint, L., Nguyen, Q. A., Roettger, C., Dixon, K., Offenbächer, M., Kohls, N., Hirsch, J., & Sirois, F. (2021b). Effectiveness of progressive muscle relaxation, deep breathing, and guided imagery in promoting psychological and physiological states of relaxation. *Evidence-Based Complementary and Alternative Medicine, 2021*(1), 1–8. https://doi.org/10.1155/2021/5924040

Weerapong, P., Hume, P. A., & Kolt, G. S. (2005). The mechanisms of massage and effects on performance, muscle recovery, and injury prevention. *Sports Medicine (Auckland, N.Z.), 35*(3), 235–256. https://doi.org/10.2165/00007256-200535030-00004

Made in the USA
Columbia, SC
04 January 2025

51019891R00080